KNITTING BY HEART

A Creative Journey for All Knitters

By Renate Hiller and Mikae Toma

© 2025 Renate Hiller and Mikae Toma

All rights reserved. No part of this publication may be reproduced, distributed, or transmitted in any form or by any means, including photocopying, recording, or other electronic or mechanical methods, without prior written permission.

ISBN 979-8-9925651-0-2

Illustrations and diagrams by Mikae Toma, except for the following:
Color wheel on page 143 courtesy Brigitte Bley-Swinston
Plant Metamorphosis on page 146 courtesy Peter Wolf
Cover and book design by Claudio Rodriguez - www.claudio-rodriguez.com
Photographs on front and back cover, and pages 5, 6, 10, 11 (left), 13 (left), 16, 17, 19, 23 (center), 29 to 33, 40, 41, 44, 46, 48, 55 (left), 57 (bottom), 62, 63, 64 (bottom), 65, 68 (bottom right), 69, 73, 77, 82 (bottom), 83 to 85, 87, 89 (right), 95, 96, 100 (top), 101 (left), 102, 104 to 107, 109, 114, 116, 117, 120, 124, 125, 127 to 132, 150, and 144 © 2025 by Claudio Rodriguez.
Photographs © 2025 by Lisa Kachajian, pages 15 (right), 64 (top), and 75 - www.lisakachajian.com
Photograph on page 98 by Dyana Van Campen
Photographs on pages 23 (top right), 52, 112, and 145 courtesy Fiber Craft Studio - fibercraftstudio.org
All other photographs are by the authors.

A portion of the revenue from the sales of this book will be donated to the Fiber Craft Studio's Applied Arts scholarship fund. The Fiber Craft Studio operates under the umbrella of the Threefold Educational Foundation and School, a 501(c)3 nonprofit organization, threefold.org.

TABLE of CONTENTS

INTRODUCTION
7_ The Fiber Crafts and Their Evolving Story
11_ Who We Are: Our Handwork Biographies
16_ How to Use Our Book

Part One: SOURCES OF INSPIRATION
20_ Rudolf Steiner, Waldorf Education, and the Handwork Curriculum
24_ The Art of Clothing—Past, Present, and Future
28_ The Wonders of Knitting

Part Two: THE KNITTING JOURNEY
42_ Recommended Ways of Working

THE PROJECTS
49_ **Spiral Gestures: Knitting in the Round**
51_ Introductory Project: Headbands
59_ From Capelet to Sweater
60_ Capelet
62_ Capelet Variation 1
63_ Capelet Variation 2
64_ Capelet Variation 3
66_ Circular Cowl
68_ Circular Cowl Variation
69_ Circular Top
73_ Circular Top Variation
74_ Extra-Warm Poncho
77_ Extra-Warm Poncho Variation
78_ Seamless Sweater
82_ Seamless Sweater Variation 1
83_ Seamless Sweater Variation 2
84_ Seamless Sweater Variation 3

85_ **Horizontal and Vertical Gestures: Knitting Back and Forth**
86_ Introductory Project: Scarves
93_ From Scarf to Jacket
94_ Long Scarf
96_ Curved Shawl
98_ Two-Shawls Vest
100_ Two-Shawls Vest Variation 1
101_ Two-Shawls Vest Variation 2
102_ Short Poncho
105_ Variation 1: Hand-spun Romney Poncho
106_ Variation 2: Linen Vest
107_ Long Vest
109_ Overlap Tunic
112_ Overlap Shoulder Vest with Haramaki
116_ Overlap Shoulder Vest Variation
117_ Loose Tunic
120_ Variation: Tunic Poncho
122_ Bolero
124_ Bolero Variation
126_ Bolero Pullover Variation 1
127_ Bolero Pullover Variation 2
128_ Hanten Jacket

Part Three: DEEPENING OUR APPRECIATION
132_ Nature's Fibers: Wool, Silk, Cotton, and Linen
138_ The Gestures and Tools of Hand-Spinning: Stick, Stone, Spindle, and Wheel
142_ The Magic of Color and the Process of Dyeing with Plants
147_ Concluding Thoughts
148_ Acknowledgments

APPENDIX
149_ Techniques
151_ Sources for Materials
Recommended Resources for Reading, Study, and Practice
152_ References

*One who works
With his hands is a laborer.
One who works with his hands
And his head is a craftsman.
One who works with his hands,
His head and his heart
Is an artist.*

— Widely attributed to Saint Francis of Assisi

The Fiber Crafts and Their Evolving Story

Greek vase, detail, around 500 BC, British Museum

The activities of spinning and weaving, together with tool making, stand at the beginning of our human journey on the earth as makers and creators.

Embedded in the great fabric of the universe, ancient peoples experienced the gods as their teachers. The myths of many cultures tell stories about the creations of the gods and their teachings to support human beings in their earthly life. In Hindu mythology, the god Mrikanda is venerated as a divine artisan primarily associated with weaving, and he is seen as a protector and inspirer of weavers. In Ancient Egypt, women learned spinning and weaving from Isis, the wife of Osiris, who was also the goddess of love and healing. Athena, the Greek goddess of wisdom, who gave the city of Athens her name, was the patron of weavers, and she herself was famed for her weaving skills. Every year the people honored her with a great festival and a procession to her temple on the Acropolis, bringing her the gift of a splendid, newly woven garment.

In North America the Navajo People became skilled weavers, since they were taught by Spider Woman, one of their Holy People, and they were taught by Earth Mother how to live in balance with nature. The collaborative work between the gods and their people is beautifully expressed in this song of the Tewa People, "Song of the Sky Loom":

> *Oh our Mother the Earth, oh our Father the Sky,*
> *Your children are we, and with tired backs*
> *We bring you the gifts that you love.*
> *Then weave for us a garment of brightness;*
> *May the warp be the white light of morning,*
> *May the weft be the red light of evening,*
> *May the fringes be the falling rain,*
> *May the border be the standing rainbow.*
> *Thus weave for us a garment of brightness*
> *That we may walk fittingly where birds sing,*
> *That we may walk fittingly where grass is green,*
> *Oh our Mother the Earth, oh our Father the Sky!*

The first artifacts made by human hands may well have been used for sacred rituals, rather than for practical purposes. By transforming earth substances, human beings participated in the wisdom of nature and learned to become makers and creators. The artifacts made by ancient peoples—which we can admire in museums around the world—speak of the sacredness of making. Whatever their use may have been, they touch us with their beauty and craftsmanship. They are gifts of nature transformed by human striving and human learning.

The craft of knitting appeared late in the human story, at a time when the old gods of mythology had receded from many people's consciousness, and the intellect was in ascendance. Although the origins of knitting are unclear, this new craft appeared in the Middle Ages in Europe and quickly spread into most households. In addition to weaving, the crossing of threads with the help of a loom, people now had a new way to make fabric: by the looping and knotting of a continuous thread with the help of knitting needles.

Handcrafts embody the great rhythms and creative gestures of the universe, shrunk to human scale to fit the human hand and teach the human mind. The rhythms of sun, moon, stars, and earth, and the rhythms governing the human body, are related to the rhythmic movements of the spinner, weaver, and knitter. Thus, they can serve us as pathways of learning and healing. The large gestures of the weaver sitting at the loom are led by the hands and involve the entire body, while the knitter performs complex movements primarily with the hands and fingers. The outer physical movements—whether large or small—go hand in hand with subtle but powerful streams of inner activity.

While ancient peoples experienced the gods as their teachers, in the Middle Ages in Europe aspiring craftsmen joined guilds to learn from human masters. The path from apprentice to journeyman to master was arduous and took many years. Aspiring journeymen had to produce "masterworks," knitted pieces demonstrating their skills. Journeymen had to travel extensively in order to learn from different masters. The third degree of training was that of master, the one who not only mastered the materials, but who acquired a certain mastery over his inner life. Practical and spiritual development went hand in hand.

While the precious pieces knit by members of the knitting guilds were used by the church and the ladies and gentlemen of the upper classes, home knitters—men and women alike—made mainly socks, caps, and mittens to keep their family members warm in winter and to make a living or garner extra income.

A totally new chapter in human development began in the middle of the eighteenth century. Led by the textile industry in Britain, the traditional craft economies in Europe, the United States, and later in Japan, were supplanted by economies based on machine manufacturing and mass production, with the rest of the countries that embraced mechanization soon following. The so-called industrial revolutions continue to bring drastic changes not only in the creation of goods, but in the quality of life to people all over the earth. Objects and materials that were once created by human hands and ensouled by a human being are now mass-produced by machines. They are easily acquired and easily disposed of. The technology that started with the making of simple tools, such as the hand-spindle, has become ever more complex, leading to computers, robots, and artificial intelligence.

These rapid developments brought many conveniences and positive changes, but also destructive forces that have damaged our natural environment and led to the exploitation of many human beings. These negative forces are so strong that the future of life on our planet is now in question. One-sided education that fosters intellectual, logical, mechanistic thinking is pushing aside holistic learning processes that work not only through the input of information, but through doing and making, practical exploring, and creative, artistic activity. A materialistic view of the world has gained the upper hand, and the living dialog between the human being and the natural world, along with ethical values that transcend this mechanistic view, have a hard struggle to be heard.

For quite some time, another revolution, or, better said, a quiet evolution has been happening, not of an industrial nature, but of a human-centered, Earth-centered nature. This evolution leads to the recognition that each human being has the capacity to contribute to the regenerative, healing processes the world needs. Toward this end, the many gifts bestowed on humanity by Rudolf Steiner at the beginning of the twentieth century are playing an important role, and the work done by countless individuals around the world gives hope and trust in the future.

The need for change and the hunger for creative activities, for making things and making them beautiful, has led to a revival of handicrafts in industrialized countries, with hand-knitting at the very forefront—now done not of necessity, but based on individual choice. Today's hand-knitters have an unprecedented abundance of materials at their disposal, countless patterns and how-to books they can learn from, and internet sites they can follow.

With our book, we seek to foster hand-knitting as a meditative practice and as a means to create beautiful, timeless pieces of clothing, not mass-produced by machine, but done with loving devotion by the individual. We see the creative, transformative process of making as a way to nurture not only the scientist but also the artist within us, and to reconnect to nature's gifts through the spirit-filled work of our hands. Rudolf Steiner held the magic wand to reopen doors to the spiritual realities of the cosmos for us modern human beings. His work has been our inspiration.

Who We Are: Our Handwork Biographies

Renate Hiller

I grew up in Ansbach, a small town in the middle of Germany, right after the Second World War. Although at that time growing food, cooking, and making and mending clothing at home were necessities, my mother and grandmother seemed to enjoy what they were doing—stitching or knitting by hand, spinning at a wheel, working in the garden, chopping vegetables, kneading dough.

I loved to participate and never grew tired of helping, making, and doing. I was extremely lucky to be guided by an inspiring teacher in our handwork classes in school, and even fantasized about becoming a handwork teacher. Although I ended up pursuing a career in publishing, I never stopped making things. Once I married and had a son and daughter, our children's Waldorf kindergarten in Heidelberg became a place where I could join other parents to make toys for the children and begin to learn about Rudolf Steiner's ideas.

After we moved to the United States, our children attended Green Meadow Waldorf School in Chestnut Ridge, New York, where I soon became an active parent. For quite a number of years, I led the parent handwork group and helped with puppet plays and handwork activities in the kindergartens, while I continued to learn about Waldorf education and the developmental stages of the growing child.

When Grete Fröhlich (1900–2001) visited our handwork group and said, "I can see you have used your hands; you need to come and work with me," I felt destiny had spoken. Of course, I agreed! Grete, who was born in Vienna, Austria, was at that time about eighty-five years old and had "retired" to the nearby Fellowship Community. She had an almost mythical reputation as a Waldorf teacher, and she was still working with adult teachers who came to her for mentoring and special counsel. Her pioneering work as teacher in several schools had been focused on the subjects of handwork, woodwork, and bookbinding, and she also had given high school courses on the history of art and architecture.

For fifteen years, until her death in 2001, I visited Grete every week, followed her instructions—which were always open-ended and required active inner and outer work on my part—and learned from her critique. As we made our way through the Waldorf handwork curriculum, I learned to read and appreciate a kind of script hidden in nature and in true art, a script of qualities that we can live into with feelings rather than simply understanding them with the intellect. In the process of making, I was engaged in a delicate inner balancing act of function and aesthetics, and I experienced with my whole being the truth and beauty of each design.

In 1989, I was asked to teach handwork courses at the Craft Studio of Sunbridge College (now Sunbridge Institute), which is devoted to Waldorf teacher education. Eventually, I gave up my career in publishing and devoted myself fully to studying at the college, teaching courses in the existing programs and offering courses and workshops to the public. Essentially, I entered into an intense path of learning and inner transformation, nurtured by amazing colleagues and by every student I taught. In 1996, we started the Applied Arts Program, a part-time program for Waldorf handwork and clay and woodwork teachers. The handwork component of this program is still offered today by the Fiber Craft Studio, which has become an independent entity under the umbrella of Threefold Educational Foundation.

When Mikae Toma came to Sunbridge College in the year 2000, her love for handwork and interest in color soon brought her to the Fiber Craft Studio as a work-study student. After several months of working together, we realized that we were meant to continue—not just for a year—but for the long term, and we do so to this day.

Today, I am living at the Fellowship Community, as Grete did during her elder years. I am still creating handwork projects and helping other elders in the community—some of them in their eighties—to rekindle their love of knitting or crocheting to make items for the annual holiday festival and craft sale. It is astonishing and touching to see how the hands and the mind and heart can embrace a path of awakening and relearning at this time of life.

Mikae Toma

When I was a young child, I saw a tree with its leaves swaying in the gentle breeze. The sunlight shone through the leaves and mysteriously revealed different shades of color. I was so deeply moved by the beauty before me that time seemed to stand still, and the sense of wonder I experienced at that moment has remained with me. Ever since, I have understood that colors in nature are not just fixed, but that there is a living reality about them, a kind of weaving between darkness and light.

As a young child growing up in a suburb of Osaka, Japan, I often played happily outside, surrounded by nature. I became very interested in working with my hands, following my mother's example in practical tasks including cooking, sewing, knitting, crocheting, embroidery, and macramé. From early on, I tried to figure out how things were made.

I do not recall who taught me how to knit, but I remember two early projects. When I was about twelve years old, I discovered how to knit seamless thumbs for mittens, just by trial and error. A few years later, I found a V-neck sweater I liked in a magazine. Intrigued by the soft edge of the neckline, once more I enjoyed the process of figuring out how to make it.

These two explorations gave me confidence and a belief that there would always be a thread of thought or inspiration that would eventually lead to good results.

At college in Japan, while majoring in early childhood education, I became interested in Waldorf education and read several books about the subject with growing enthusiasm. After working as a kindergarten teacher for several years, I moved to Germany and participated in a two-year course for Waldorf early childhood educators. The rhythms of life in the kindergarten and the artistic quality permeating the play areas and the activities with the children opened my heart to experiencing the world in new ways.

My yearning to know more about color, especially plant colors, along with the role of handwork in life and in the environment, led me to enroll in Foundation Studies at Sunbridge College, a one-year preparatory course for the Waldorf teacher education program, where I met Renate Hiller. When I became engaged in the projects that Renate had given me—together with written indications by Rudolf Steiner—my soul seemed to sing and dance. I soon realized that I had met my life's work!

Renate supported me fully in my initial explorations and we developed a harmonious way of collaborating that continues to this day. In 2014—after sixteen years abroad—I moved back to my native country, Japan, with a mission in my heart: to bring the practical and soul/spiritual aspects of artistic handwork to the people here.

As I share what I have learned with the students who attend my classes, the words Renate once wrote in an essay continue to inspire me:

> Today, more than ever, the crafts have the mission to reconnect the human being to the Earth and her substances, bring healing to the senses and the soul, and foster the creative capacities of the human being.

Our Journey Together

Our journey together evolved in exciting and stimulating ways and led to many new initiatives, with the help of colleagues, friends, and volunteers. In addition to running the studio, caring for the dye garden, and our ongoing teaching, we tried to make time in our busy schedules for study, handwork practice, and research. As we returned to "the source," studying Rudolf Steiner's pedagogical lectures and indications for handwork classes given to the teachers of the first Waldorf School in Stuttgart, Germany, and the Friedward Schule in Dornach, Switzerland, we encountered his call to bring renewing impulses to the art of clothing. This call kept resonating in our hearts and minds and seemed to intensify, until we decided to take it up as a central research question: How can we create pieces of clothing, based on a spiritual view of the human being, that are both functional and beautiful and fit into the culture of today? This was the central question we came to, and it felt like a huge task, a tremendous challenge!

Rudolf Steiner's design sketches (see "Steiner's Sketches," page 21) and the work done by the handwork teachers and children in early Waldorf schools became a special source of inspiration.

We also explored the gestures and qualities of garments made and worn by people in ancient cultures, and were much taken by the simplicity of the designs and their meaningful embellishments. These garments seemed to be an outer expression of the soul/spiritual connections between people, a representation of their cultural identity.

On a practical level, we did not have to think very long about the choice of materials or techniques, soon deciding that knitting was our preferred choice. Although knitting is often seen as a head-directed activity, where the knitter follows an existing pattern and is concerned chiefly with measurements and numbers, we developed a meditative way of working, a creative process of wholeness. Artistic choices about color, form, and texture could be made at every step, with our bodies serving as our "pattern."

We chose natural and—wherever possible—organic fibers for their health-giving quality and their low impact on the environment. We further enhanced their healing qualities by hand-dyeing our yarns with plant colors, many of them gathered in the surrounding countryside or in the garden beds. For a number of our pieces, we hand-spun the yarns using fleeces from local farms and dyed them with plants from the garden. This holistic sheep-to-shawl approach is the most satisfying, as it offers complete creative freedom and is truly friendly to the environment.

With every piece we made, we strove for an organic quality in our designs; function and beauty needed to be brought into a harmonious relationship. This harmonious interplay is a signature of nature and can be observed all around us, including in our own physical body.

As we became ever more involved in this work, the making of garments and the process of knitting became a daily practice, a living, creative process that took on more and more meaning. The process itself became as important as the finished piece. For several years, we spent most evenings, weekends, and a good part of our vacations immersed in joyous, and sometimes intense, knitting explorations. As we strove to create harmonious color conversations and beautiful textures in line with the overall designs, we gradually built skills and capacities. Filled with gratitude for nature's gifts and the creative capacities growing in us, we fell in love with what we were doing.

Every so often we got together for a session of "show-and-tell," when a finished piece was introduced, tried on, scrutinized, and mostly admired. These were much-cherished moments of exchange and inspiration, when we shared questions, concerns, and insights with each other and often with our colleagues and students. During one of these sessions the idea for this book was born, a new project that would allow us to share the riches we had encountered on our journey with readers far and wide.

The research and writing for this book evolved over many years, punctuated by active times and times of rest according to outer circumstances in our lives. One of these "times of rest" came about through a fire in one of the houses at the Fellowship Community, which destroyed most of Renate's belongings, including her knitted samples and notebooks. It was thanks to the strength of the Fellowship Community and the love and generosity of family, friends, and countless other people that Renate could soon reorient herself in life. Thanks to her Fiber Craft Studio friends, the reknitting of the lost garments was accomplished. The meetings at the Fiber Craft Studio—with Mikae joining online from Japan—not only led to new garments, made lovingly in the spirit of research, but resulted in beautiful design variations that have greatly enriched the offerings in this book.

With the publication of this book, we invite you, dear knitters, to collaborate with us, becoming fellow travelers on a transformative journey.

—Renate Hiller and Mikae Toma

How To Use Our Book

We hope this book will become a trusted companion and resource on your journey, whether you are new to hand-knitting or you have been "on the road" for many years. We encourage you to work with a mood of gratitude and loving attention while you hone your skills, deepen your knowledge, and create unique pieces of clothing. The book is divided into three main parts, rounded out by introductory texts, concluding thoughts, acknowledgments, and an appendix.

Part One, "Sources of Inspiration": This provides insights into Rudolf Steiner's life and Waldorf education, the art of clothing in the past, present, and future, and the wonders of knitting.

Part Two, "The Knitting Journey": This begins with "Recommended Ways of Working" and contains the main knitting designs and their variations.

In this core section of the book, we have presented our designs according to two basic ways of knitting: knitting in the round, with its spiral movements, and knitting back and forth, with the emphasis on horizontal and vertical movements. Both sections open with an introductory project, a warm-up exploration: headbands for knitting in the round, and scarves for knitting back and forth.

After the introductory projects, the knitted designs follow a kind of natural growth process. A capelet lengthens and becomes a tunic; the tunic grows arms and becomes a sweater; the scarf widens and becomes a poncho, and so on. This is the organic, step-by-step process we ourselves followed as we developed our designs.

You are welcome to join us on the entire journey, or follow partway and knit any piece or a few pieces that speak to you. Of course, you need to take your background and skill level into consideration as you make your choices. Although the basic, organic shapes are all easy to make and personalize, there is a progression from one design to the next in terms of the time, energy, and skill level required. Whatever you choose to do, be sure to first knit some of the relevant introductory projects; they are meant to serve as orientation pieces.

Part Three, "Deepening Our Appreciation": This starts with an introduction to the main natural fibers. We then give an overview of basic hand-spinning techniques, with drawings and photos to illustrate how, with simple tools, a cosmic twist can be added to the fibers of the earth. We end with an exploration of the mysteries of color and a glimpse of plant-dyeing techniques, richly illustrated with photos from our work. Each theme can be

explored further using resources listed in the appendix, and we hope you will be inspired to delve further into the ones that touch your creative soul.

The yarns we have used can be found in any knitting shop, at a local farm or farmer's market, or among your supplies at home. We also include our suggested sources for yarn in the appendix. What makes our yarns extra special are the plant colors with which we have dyed them. These beautiful colors are living food for our soul and a therapy for the senses, which nowadays tend to be undernourished or over-bombarded. We recommend that you try working with plant-dyed yarns, and maybe even experiment with plant dyeing yourself, to experience the nourishing qualities of plant colors.

Sun Dye Jars

Design Components

You will meet and get to know each design in a variety of ways:

Main Photo: The design worn by Mikae, Renate, or a friend, sometimes accompanied by additional photos showing details of the design or aspects of the process of making on the subsequent pages.

Since Renate's original pieces that were lost in the fire were not photographed by a professional, they are depicted in a small format. The replacement pieces, which are not copies but variations done in the spirit of research by Renate and friends from the Fiber Craft Studio, were professionally photographed and are shown in a larger format.

Short Introduction: Key features and functional aspects of the project as it was originally developed.

Personal Stories: A description of the creative process from the idea to the finished piece; the stories also include helpful hints and recommendations.

Materials and Tools: Information about the yarns, including fiber content, approximate yardage and gauge; needle type, size, and length; and recommendations for color, including notes about the color design and natural dyes used for the piece as shown in the main photo.

Schematic Drawings: A two-dimensional rendering of each design, including the overall dimensions (in inches), the knitting direction, the number of stitches cast on, increases and decreases, and some structural elements, such as purl rows in a knitted texture (where applicable). The overall dimension and stitch numbers are for women's sizes small to medium. For smaller and larger sizes, the dimensions and stitch numbers can simply be decreased or increased based on stitch gauge swatches and measurements of the body. Frequent trying on of the evolving piece is always recommended. In some cases, additional helpful guidelines for size adjustments are given.

Instructions: Step-by-step guidance through the process of knitting the main piece, in the size shown in the photos. These instructions provide additional help for knitters who might struggle otherwise. In the process of working with this book, you might be able to refer less and less to the instructions. Instead, you may find yourself able to create a piece based on the photo, schematic drawing, and other information given.

Size Adjustment: Helpful guidelines to adjust for different gauges or larger or smaller sizes.

Design Variations: A photo, short descriptive text, and sometimes an outline drawing highlight variations to the basic design. These variations can form a basis for your own creativity and decision-making—and your own unique designs.

This multifaceted presentation of each piece forms an organic whole, providing you with the information you need to progress with your knitting, stimulate your creativity, and spark new ideas.

Part One:
Sources of Inspiration

Rudolf Steiner, Waldorf Education, and the Handwork Curriculum

What is the essential nature of the human being? What is the relationship of our planet, Earth, to the cosmos? How can we prepare for a future of brotherhood, equality, and inner freedom in social life? These are just a few of the important questions Rudolf Steiner explored throughout his life.

We learned about Rudolf Steiner when we encountered Waldorf education, Mikae as a kindergarten teacher in Japan, and Renate as a mother of two children in Germany. We were both drawn to this education because it is totally child-centered, with the healthy development of body, soul, and spirit of each child as its primary objective. We both felt touched by the beauty, order, and harmony in the classroom spaces, the mood of loving-kindness permeating the school community, and the holistic quality of the curriculum, with its rigorous and artistic approach to teaching.

Rudolf Steiner spent much of his life writing, lecturing, and creating pieces of art in service of human development and the renewal of human culture. By developing and maintaining the disciplined inquiry of a scientist, the clear thinking of a philosopher, and the expanding consciousness of an artist and spiritual investigator, he was able to perceive and investigate spiritual realities underlying the physical world as we know it.

He was born in 1861 in Croatia (which was then part of the Austro-Hungarian Empire) and died in 1925 in Switzerland, a few years after the end of the First World War. In his autobiography, *Mein Lebensgang* (My Life's Path), he describes the bucolic landscape of mountains, forests, meadows, and fields that surrounded him as he was growing up. His mother was a homemaker and his father worked for the railroad, first as a telegraph operator and then as a station master. As a young boy, Steiner was fascinated by the railroad and the technical innovations of the time, including the telegraph. He was less excited about the lessons presented in the rural one-room schoolhouses he attended in his early school years; so, he pursued extracurricular studies in geometry, German literature, and philosophy, often with the help of a teacher or family friend. By the time he attended a science-based high school in the outskirts of Vienna, he was tutoring classmates and younger students, and during his studies at the Technical University in Vienna he was hired as a tutor by a family with four children, one of them with special needs. In this way, he gained experience as a teacher early on in life.

After his formal education, which also included a doctorate in philosophy from the University of Rostock in Germany, Steiner became a well-known figure in the literary, philosophical, intellectual circles of middle Europe. For the body of his work and philosophical and practical approach to life, he coined the term "anthroposophy" (from the Greek: Anthropos, the human being, and Sophia, wisdom). As a spiritual teacher, he inspired many individuals to find new meaning and direction in life by taking up the study of anthroposophy and a conscious practice of self-development in service to the world.

Rudolf Steiner's influence continues to reverberate worldwide, and many individuals are making meaningful choices in daily life, inspired by his ideas. Waldorf schools, Camphill communities, biodynamic farms, and many other initiatives are key manifestations of his vision of a human community dedicated to service rather than personal gain, and ultimately to the pursuit of truth, beauty, and goodness, which he believed to be the highest ideals of human striving.

Waldorf Education and the Handwork Curriculum

> The need for imagination, a sense of truth, and a feeling for responsibility, these are the three forces that constitute the nerves of education.
>
> —Rudolf Steiner, *The Foundations of Human Experience*

Rudolf Steiner founded the first Waldorf School in Stuttgart, Germany, in 1919, at the request of Emil Molt, owner of the Waldorf cigarette factory. Together with the teachers, he developed an artistic way of teaching according to the developmental stages of the child, and a curriculum relatively free from the involvement of the state. It was through the education of children that he wanted to plant seeds for a renewal of human culture. Today, there are more than a thousand Waldorf schools in sixty-four countries worldwide, as well as nearly two thousand Waldorf kindergartens, preschools, and childcare centers.

From the start, the Waldorf curriculum included lessons in artistic handwork for all children. Under the guidance of Hedwig Hauck, the handwork teacher at the first school in Stuttgart, the children learned to knit, crochet, sew, and embroider, in order to make useful and beautiful items for daily life. At the Friedwartschule, a school for children fourteen years and older, founded by Rudolf Steiner in 1921 in Dornach, Switzerland, much emphasis was placed on embellishing items for the home and pieces of clothing by using fabric paints and embroidery. The handwork classes were guided by the painter Louise van Blommestein, with Steiner as a frequent visitor. For all handwork projects, he stressed the need to bring beauty and function into a harmonious interplay, relating everything to the human being as well as to the surroundings. During his pedagogical lectures and in the classroom, Steiner drew schematic sketches to illustrate the essence of these design principles. Van Blommestein also sketched designs based on these principles. These sketches point to embellishments that are not decorative in an arbitrary way, but relate fully to the function of the objects and to the realities of life.

Steiner's Sketches

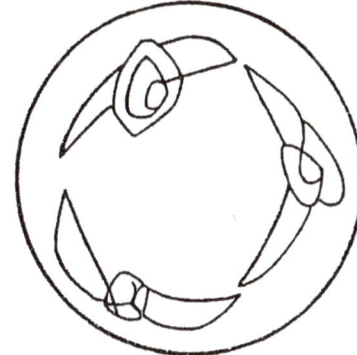 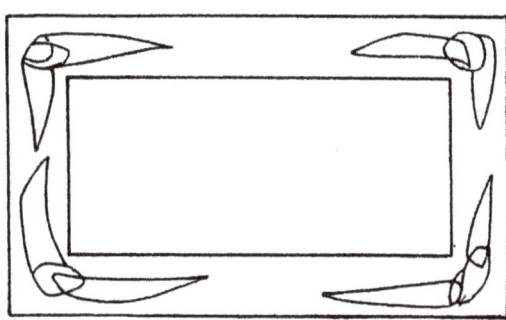

Schematic sketches for embroidery designs for tablecloths for a round table with 3 legs and a rectangular table with 4 legs

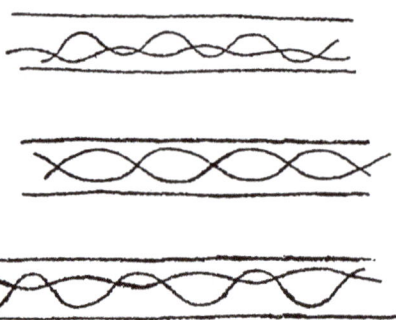

Schematic sketches for embroidery designs for dresses

With the design sequences for dresses, Steiner introduced qualitative changes of form. In the center (around the waist), the forms are balanced and symmetrical below and above the imagined mid-line; around the neck or collar there is an upward and open movement in the forms; and at the bottom they express a downward pull or a kind of closure. Yet in their essential nature these forms are related to each other, as the leaf of a plant is related to the flower.

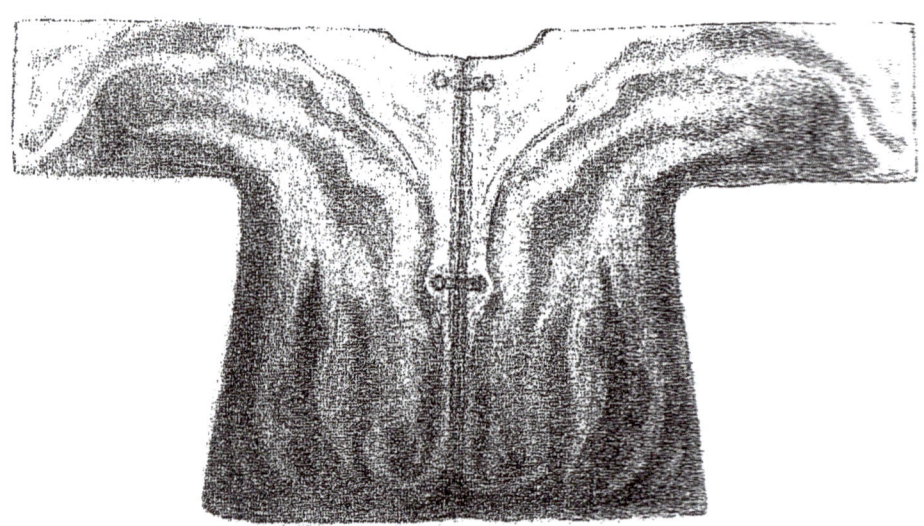

Van Blommestein communicated her ideas about painting on fabric in these sketches of a jacket and shawl.

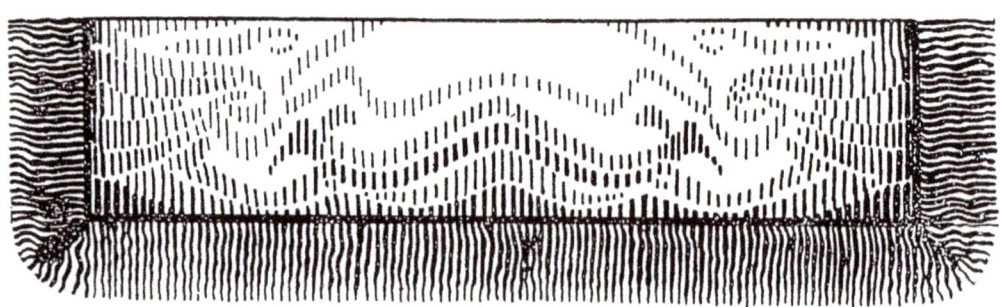

Van Blommestein's sketches illustrate metamorphic changes with regard to darkness and light. The light tones toward the top and center of the shawl and of the jacket emerge in an organic way from the darkness at the bottom. The changes are gradual and have a living quality about them. In the design for the shawl the lightest tones are around the neck, and in the jacket they are close to the face and hands. These qualitative changes point to the soul/spiritual, light-filled nature of the human being that we can perceive most strongly around the head, face, and hands. At the bottom the garments also relate to the earth, and toward the top to the realms of air and light.

In visiting children and teachers in the classroom, Steiner often conveyed the message that everything they created should be as meaningful and organic as if grown out of the object itself, as mentioned by Louise van Blommestein in her small book *Künstlerische Handarbeiten* (Artistic Handwork). Steiner repeatedly called for a "renewal of the art of clothing," which in his view had become no art at all.

In Waldorf schools around the world today, this impulse for renewal is explored in handwork classes. First-graders learn to knit back and forth with two needles. As fifth graders, children manipulate four or five needles to knit socks, mittens, hats, and other pieces for their wardrobe. They sew (and sometimes embroider) some of their own clothing in the upper grades.

First Grade projects, Applied Arts Program, Fiber Craft Studio

Fifth Grade student projects

The children are guided by handwork teachers in making judgments about materials, colors, forms, and textures, with the aim of creating beautiful and useful pieces that they love and can be proud of. Along the way—while they are engaged with their hands, hearts, and minds to transform gifts from nature—they are developing their own potentialities. In the creative process they learn to be attentive, to practice patience and perseverance, and to develop a sense for the practical and a love for beauty.

> Children who learn while they are young to make practical things by hand in an artistic way, and for the benefit of others as well as for themselves, will not be strangers to life or to other people when they are older. They will be able to form their lives and their relationships in a social and artistic way, so that their lives are thereby enriched.
>
> —Hedwig Hauck

The Art of Clothing – Past, Present, and Future

In the heart feeling moves,
In the head thinking shines,
In the limbs willing rules.
Weaving illumination,
Strength of the weaving,
Illuminating strength:
This is the human being.

—Rudolf Steiner, "Ecce Homo"

In order to thrive, we human beings need layers of protection. First, we develop in our mother's womb; then we are swaddled and cradled, and we grow up sheltered in a house, a hut, or a cave. As adults, we continue to need layers of protection to create an environment that is just right for us, not too hot and not too cold. The right pieces of clothing—the layers next to our skin—play a paramount role in keeping us well protected and healthy.

However, in order to satisfy a longing in the deeper layers of our nature, the purely functional purpose of clothing—that of protection—needs to be complemented by something else: the element of beauty.

The beauty of nature delights us when we stop to look at the flowers, butterflies, trees, and meadows, taking in their living colors, forms, and movements. When we encounter harmony of beauty and function, for example in a piece of clothing that was created with our loving attention, it touches us deeply. We feel acknowledged and spoken to as human beings; our higher nature—that part in us that seeks to serve the good—resonates in sympathy, and our bodily nature experiences a sense of heightened well-being.

Today, most clothing is manufactured by the global fashion industry, with the primary objective of financial gain. Although fair labor practices have been adopted by some companies and "upcycling" has become a buzzword, unfair practices and environmental degradation continue to prevail in the global production chain. Through advertising, companies seek to exploit the longing for beauty by stimulating the desire for change, irrespective of the real needs of the human being.

In ancient cultures, common forms of dress arose from spiritual insight, had special meaning for the people, and were closely linked to their identity. All people of the same folk, the same clan, wore the same style of dress—a style that expressed and grew out of their common nature, experiences, and environment. Throughout history and in all cultures, clothing has also been used to denote a person's rank, social status, and position in society, and some pieces of clothing were reserved for special occasions and for ceremonial purposes only.

According to Rudolf Steiner, as discussed in the book *Elephants to Einstein*, three basic forms of dress evolved under the guidance of spiritual leaders, which were related to the threefold nature of the human being. Head, trunk, and limbs gave rise to the cloak, the tunic, and the loincloth.

Cloak

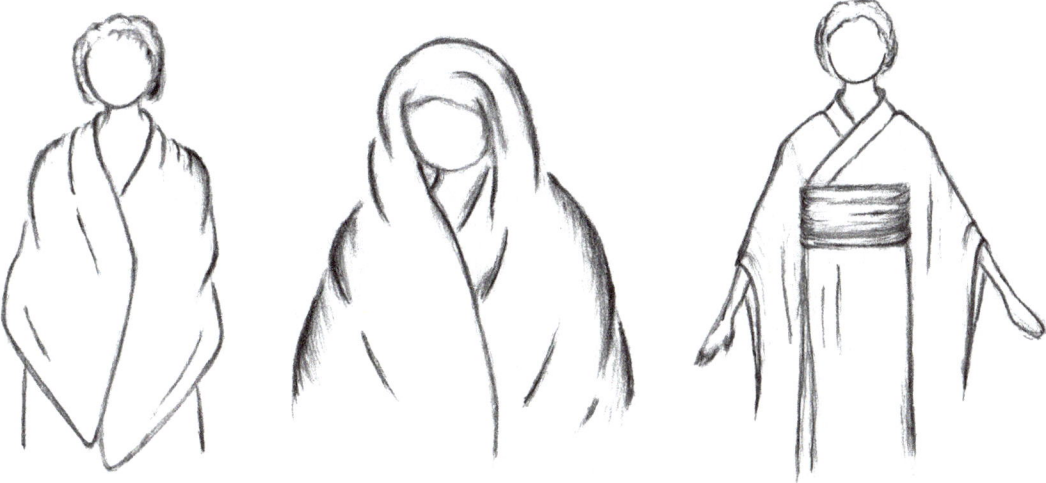

The cloak was originally not only thrown over the shoulders but also covered the head, the seat of our nerve-sense and thinking activity. It is placed on the head or the shoulders by a sweeping circular motion of both arms, and held in the front either with both hands or by knotting or fastening the two sides in other ways. Simple versions of this garment are rectangular blankets or pieces of fabric, a handy and versatile covering still used all over the world. The Japanese kimono is an interesting version of this garment. Essentially made out of four woven panels, it is brought over the shoulders to the front, with the left side crossing over the right side. All capes, jackets, coats, vests, and cardigans are related to this garment, and so are hoods and other forms of head coverings.

Tunic

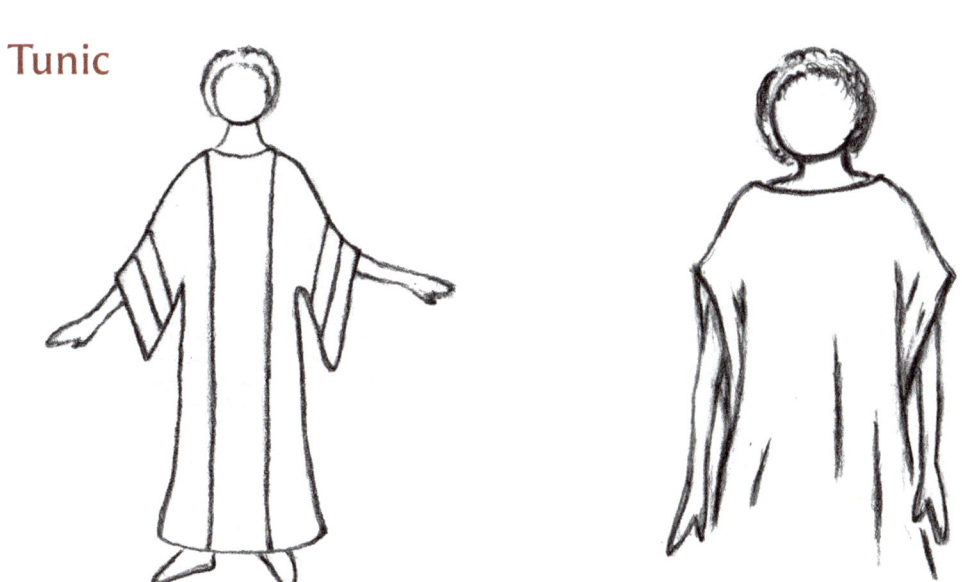

The tunic was developed as a covering for the chest area, the seat of our feeling life, with its inner rhythms of heartbeat and breathing. In general, tunics are placed on the body

THE ART OF CLOTHING

from above; hanging from the shoulders, they cover the front and back of the body. The tunic became a basic piece of clothing in the ancient Near East and Eastern Mediterranean cultures. A look at its name in different languages indicates its widespread appeal: in Hebraic, kethoneth; in Greek, chiton; in Latin, tunica; in Arabic, quoton. The dalamatica, a special tunic with colored bands emphasizing symmetry and uprightness, evolved in the Eastern Roman Empire with the spread of Christianity. It was later adopted by the Christian priesthood, medieval knights, and religious orders. The caftan (a word of Persian origin) has been worn by many cultures in the Middle East and Africa for thousands of years. Other versions of the tunic became widespread in the Americas; the traditional dresses and shirts of the indigenous cultures of North America are still worn today during ceremonial gatherings, and in Mexico and the Andean mountains, we can admire the ponchos and huipils made out of one, two, or three woven pieces. All dresses and pullover sweaters are related to this garment.

Apron

The loincloth or apron was originally developed to cover and give expression to the limbs, with their outer movements imbued by our will-nature. To create the most basic form of this garment, fabric is wrapped around the lower body, with one end tucked in at the waist. In the distant past, more complex forms evolved that included the arms, or at least one arm, by winding the fabric further up the chest. Ancient Babylonian sculptures and cylinder seals show examples of these more complex versions. The loincloth was worn by men in Ancient Egypt, as well as in the ancient Inca and Aztec cultures. Native American cultures developed leggings and breechcloths from animal skins. In modern-day India, Mahatma Gandhi wore the simple loincloth, called dhoti, and spun the yarn used to weave it. The sari, a six-yard-long piece of fabric, is worn by women in India to this day. Our skirts, trousers, pants, and leggings are related to this garment, and our modern-day wrap-skirts are their closest cousins.

As we can see, early forms of dress were made out of one or several panels of fabric or animal skins and loosely wrapped around or draped over the body. The fabric was not cut, except maybe to create an opening for the head. The practice of cutting fabric into pieces and sewing them together to closely fit the form of the human body evolved in medieval Europe, together with the profession of the tailor.

According to Rudolf Steiner, the beautiful European folk costumes are the last remnants of clothing made in Europe that were originally inspired by spiritual insight. Lovingly made by hand, they were treasured for their meaningful designs and embellishments. They expressed the spiritual ties that held people together and contributed to a group's identity. Today, these costumes are mostly worn on special occasions to keep up a sense of tradition, or they can be admired in museum exhibits as relics of the past.

In North America, individual Native American tribes developed their own distinctive styles of dress. Clothes, headdresses, and ornamentation were closely linked to tribal identity, clan backgrounds, and sacred beliefs.

The clothing arts—as all forms of art—are a kind of script that traces the evolution of human consciousness. Tremendous changes have occurred in human development, moving from the group identity of early cultures to the modern individual seeking personal freedom. The dream quality of mythological consciousness, with its sense of oneness with the world and the divine, has metamorphosed into a tendency for one-sided intellectual thinking and a growing sense of alienation.

By means of his books, lectures, and works of art, Rudolf Steiner sought to re-enliven our relationship to the cosmos and to open a path of renewal for the modern human being. It is not a question of copying the past, but of embracing the journey of our evolving humanity while imbuing the present and preparing for the future with spiritual insights available to us now.

Spiritual insights, practical considerations, and a wish to create health-giving sheaths for the human being of today may help us in planting seeds for a new art of clothing. Our research is a modest attempt in this direction.

The Wonders of Knitting
Some Thoughts and Practical Explorations

> Today there are only a few . . . who recognize how much the ability to knit can help toward healthy thinking and healthy logic.
>
> —Rudolf Steiner, *The Child's Changing Consciousness*

Wool, silk, cotton, linen, and many other fibers are gifts from the natural world that beckon to be transformed into beautiful sheaths for human beings, supporting our survival and enhancing the comfort of our homes.

During the Middle Ages, knitting evolved most likely out of braiding, tying of knots, and nålbinding, crafts that had accompanied humanity for millennia, together with spinning and weaving. This simple new "technology"—using two sticks and a length of fiber to create fabric—brought with it unlimited creative possibilities for the individual artisan and the guilds guiding the development of this work. Although, with the spread of machine knitting, hand-knitting seems less necessary, modern hand knitters continue to derive great satisfaction from this tactile practice.

What is the magic of this activity that is loved by so many people?

Hand-knitting is slow and rhythmical; our left and right hands work harmoniously together to create a fabric out of a continuous strand of fiber. With the help of knitting needles, we make loops and lace them into each other to create rows of stitches that form an organic structure, a flexible fabric.

Within the knitting texture, everything flows in soft waves and curves. Although we speak of rows and ribs, pointing to linear aspects, these rows and ribs have a living, dynamic quality; they are never stiff.

With flexible fingers, we can learn knitting rather quickly, since there are only two basic stitches: knit and purl. To create these stitches, we move our hands somewhat differently, but if we look carefully at the fabric we create, we see that a knit stitch on the front side of the knitting is a purl stitch in the back, and vice versa. These two stitches are actually one and the same, seen from two different sides, like two sides of a coin. To create a rectangular or square piece of knitting, we need to learn only two additional skills: casting on to begin, and binding off to finish. Increasing and decreasing are skills that enable us to change the

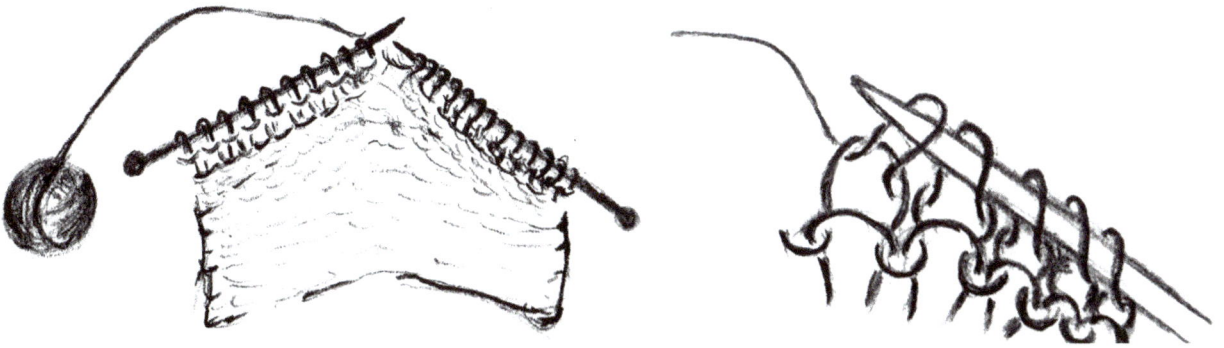

shape of a piece: to make a piece wider, we increase the number of stitches, and to make it narrower, we decrease the number.

Unraveling the fabric is almost as magical as creating it. All it takes is a tug. We pull on a yarn-end and voilà, stitch by stitch, we can easily unravel the whole piece … or a few stitches … or a few rows. The quality of the entire structure depends on the quality of each individual stitch, because each stitch holds all the other stitches. The chain comes to mind: one weak link and the quality of the whole chain suffers. The interdependence of all life forms also comes to mind, the reality that organisms live in relationship with one another and with their surroundings in a closely knit ecosystem, a supportive network.

The introduction of color is as easy as making stitches. We simply use colored yarns of our choice. We can change colors anywhere we would like; the possibilities are endless.

Detail from Capelet Variation 3

Hand-knitting allows us to work in truly ecological ways by sourcing yarns from local farmers or by buying a whole fleece and spinning and dyeing the yarns ourselves. Knitting allows us to work with zero waste. Even small, leftover yarn-ends can be unraveled and felted to make buttons or small mats, or we can collect them and use them as stuffing for pillows or handmade toys.

Even when we use manufactured yarn, rather than hand-spun, knitting a garment with our hands is a deed with many positive implications and results.

Rudolf Steiner has likened human work done with thread, especially knitting, to the cosmic knitting of the stars and to the knitting of thoughts in the human being. The planets, in their journeys around the sun as seen from the earth, inscribe "all manner of marvelous loopings and rhythmical patterns"—to quote Dr. Hermann von Baravalle, one of the first teachers in the Waldorf school in Stuttgart, Germany, in his book *Die Erscheinungen am Sternenhimmel* (Configurations in the Starry Heavens).

In the human realm, the rhythmic and repetitive movements of both hands, with left and right hands working together and the needles crossing again and again, stimulate the brain and support the development of mobile thinking.

The movements of the hands, working in unison with the mind and the heart, involve the whole human being in an act of creation that is unique and immensely satisfying and that can be a therapeutic treatment for many ailments typical of our time.

When we sit down with our knitting and begin to converse with our materials, we enter a special place of relaxation; the rest of the world seems to recede, as we become attentive and fully present in the moment, experiencing the magic of creation. Stitch by stitch, row by row, from the realm of imagination, something tangible comes into being. As we work consciously with the materials, the stitches, and the colors, a kind of alchemy happens between us and our piece. We meet the qualities inherent in the materials, and we meet our own special gifts and limitations. As the piece unfolds, we may encounter challenges, even moments of despair, but above all there are the joy and satisfaction of being in the moment, of handling something beautiful, of persevering and achieving amazing results. With every new creation, we engage in an act of courage, a journey of transformation.

Along the way, we may become aware of the magical relationship between knit and purl stitches. A knit stitch in front of the knitting has the shape of a slightly curved "V"; in the back it is a purl stitch, a plump, somewhat curved horizontal dash. What we are actually seeing are different parts of the same loop. An overall knit stitch texture (with knit rows on the front side of the knitting and purl rows on the back) is called "stockinette" or "stocking

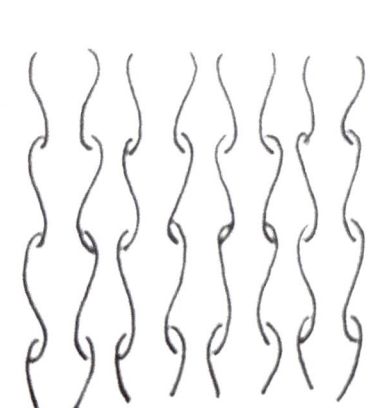

Stockinette; detail from Seamless Sweater Variation 2

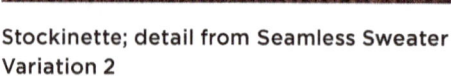

stitch." It has a smooth, even surface with the V-shaped stitches arranged in vertical linear formations.

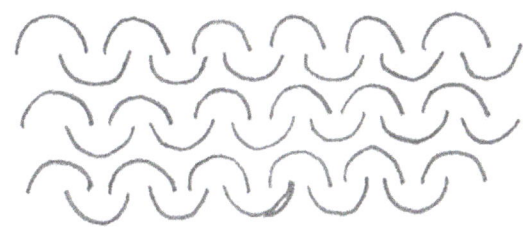

Reverse stockinette; detail from reverse side of Seamless Sweater Variation 2

The reverse of this, an overall purl stitch texture (sometimes called "reverse stockinette"), looks and feels somewhat bumpy, with the stitches interlacing in a horizontal manner. The edges of a stockinette piece tend to roll in a soft curve, once the stitches have been bound off: along the sides they will roll toward the back, and on the top and bottom edges toward the front.

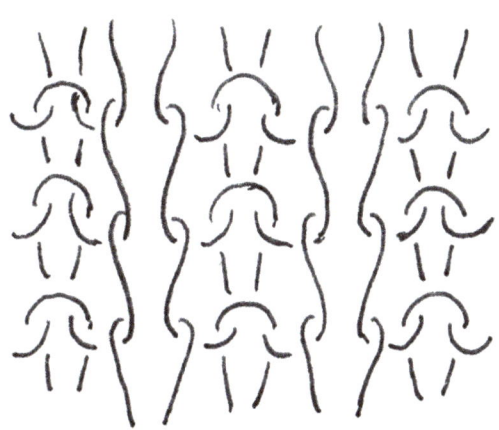

Ribbing, k1 p1; detail from Headband Variation 2

When we place knit and purl stitches side by side, they actually pull and curve in different directions. This alternation of tension adds flexibility. A ribbed piece of knitting, which alternates knit and purl stitches over a number of rows, creates extra stretch, such as is needed for cuffs.

THE WONDERS OF KNITTING

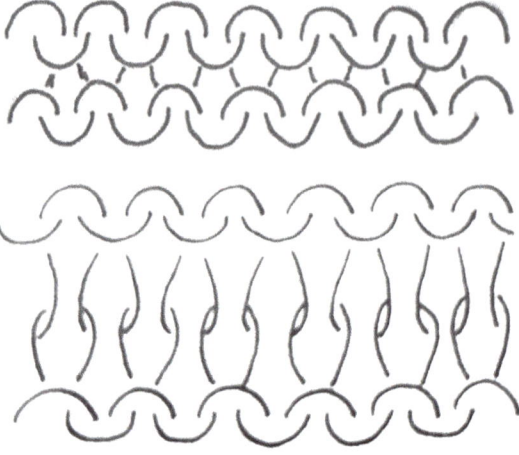

Garter stitch texture | **Garter stitch texture, when stretched**

A garter stitch is created by knitting every row, when knitting back and forth. To create a garter stitch texture in circular knitting, rounds of knit stitches alternate with rounds of purl stitches. Garter stitch enhances overall flexibility, and the edges of the knitted fabric do not roll.

Into an overall stockinette texture we can insert one or more purl rows for extra stretch, for example in the area of the shoulders, where lots of movement is happening. These inserted purl rows not only increase flexibility, they are also more prominent and feel heavier than knit rows. With a dynamic increase of widening purl bands across a piece of knitting, such as a sweater, we can introduce the quality of increasing heaviness.

On the other hand, purl ribs that are inserted in a vertical direction will accentuate uprightness and strength.

Edges rolling toward the back; details from the Long Vest

Edges rolling toward the front; detail from Headband Variation 2

Edges that roll toward the back add to the qualities of softness and fullness, and edges that roll toward the front across a finished piece of knitting form a beautiful curve and give a sense of openness.

Colors have magical relationships as well, and we have personal relationships with them. We may choose colors simply because we like them, or because they harmonize with our complexion or with other pieces in our wardrobe. As we lovingly work with them, they may reveal their special qualities, their inner nature, to us, and we may discover aspects of our inner nature through them.

Colors weave between polarities of harmony and disharmony, darkness and light, heaviness and lightness, warmth and coolness. For example, with warm reds and oranges, we can knit the quality of a warm heart into a sweater. Quiet blues will lend themselves to a calming layer of protection, while shining yellows may bring lightness and joy close to a face. The possibilities for creative discovery are unlimited.

As we focus with loving attention on the interplay of stitches and colors to bring changes of a metamorphic nature into the design of our piece, in harmony with its purpose, we are pursuing a path of apprenticeship and developing the capacities for qualitative perception and for empathy. As these capacities grow in us, we become better equipped to read the book of nature and the hearts of our fellow human beings.

When we hold a finished piece in our hands—it may be as small as a little pouch or as large as a sweater—we are thankful for gifts we have received through the process of making. It is more than merely an object; it embodies a journey of transformation, it is a gift of nature imbued with human striving, and it is a contribution to a sustainable way of life.

Knitting Small Pouches

With this practical exploration, Mikae shows how much one can learn by knitting a variety of small pouches. She illustrates how knit and purl stitches can be used to achieve a harmonious interplay of form and color, with the aim of balancing aspects of function and beauty in the finished piece. A pouch is a good introduction to knitting. It is quick and satisfying, and a wonderful use for yarn left over from other projects.

The purpose of a small pouch is to hold and protect a small item. A small pouch can also be put into a larger bag.

By creating a pouch for one of your belongings, you may learn to pay closer attention to the objects around you, including where you put them and how you care for them. If you really delve into the use and purpose of a pouch, you will experience the many considerations to be pondered in the creative process of any knitting project, no matter the size. The essence of our way of working is all there.

A pouch has an opening, where an item can go in and out, and a compartment, where the item is to be held. It also has a front and a back, and it can have a flap to cover the opening. Along with the flap, a closure is needed for security. When we hold a filled pouch in our hand, there is also a sense of top and bottom. The opening is at the top, and the closed compartment at the bottom, holding the object so it doesn't fall out.

There are many considerations in choosing colors for a pouch. We tend to choose colors according to our likes and dislikes, but it is worthwhile to ponder other aspects. Do we choose a medium blue because we want to emphasize a quality of holding or protecting, or do we choose a bright red that makes it easy to find the pouch in our bag? The colors can also be chosen in relation to the object that will go inside. They could be similar to the object that will go into the pouch, or complementary, to make the object stand out. If several colors are chosen, we can ask ourselves how they relate to each other. Are they from the same color family, or are they harmonious for other reasons? If two colors are chosen, as in our little projects, is it clear which one is lighter and which one is darker, and where do we place the lighter color and where the darker?

There are many different ways to create knitted pouches, but in order to clarify the intentions here, we have kept it simple. We offer two designs, both knitted with a worsted-weight three-ply yarn in two colors, one lighter and one darker.

Please study the drawings and photos and follow Mikae's descriptions to create these two types of pouches.

Simple Knit Stitch Version (Garter Texture)

Mikae Toma

This very simple knitted pouch is created with the knit stitch only, which creates a garter stitch texture when knitting back and forth. The conscious use of two colors makes the creative process and the finished pouch special.

The width and length are determined by the object that goes inside. This pouch was made for my small square compact mirror.

I decided to use the darker color for the main body of the pouch because it expresses a gesture of protection and of holding, and to use the lighter color for the flap at the top. I also tried to achieve an organic transition between the darker and lighter colors.

After I had determined the width of the pouch, I started knitting with the darker color, until the knitting was long enough to hold my object well when folded up. I consciously followed the knitting process with my imagination, always picturing the section of the pouch where I was knitting. I started with the edge that would become the opening on the front side of the pouch. I knitted down the front, then the bottom, and finally up the back section. As I came close to the top of the back side, I gradually brought in the lighter color to create a transition between the holding gesture of the pouch and the more open and active gesture of the flap. A row or two of the lighter color is knitted in between rows of the darker color, before changing completely to the lighter color.

It is very subtle but interesting to see the transition from the darker to the lighter color; you will notice that the color changes occur differently on the two sides of the fabric. When you sew the piece together, you can make a decision as to which side of the knitting you would like to have on the outside. There is no right or wrong. There is only a qualitative difference, and you can make a choice, as you look at the whole design.

This transitional section leads to the flap. I created the flap's triangular shape by decreasing 1 stitch at the beginning of each row until 5 stitches were left. I bound off these stitches relatively tightly to form the base of the loop for the button. To complete the loop, I added a few tight chain stitches with a crochet hook and secured the yarn end in the bound-off stitches with a sewing needle.

After sewing the sides together, again looking at the whole, I asked myself where the button should be placed and how big to make it, so it would go easily through the loop. I made the button by felting teased-out yarn-ends from the knitting, aiming to achieve harmony in the materials and colors.

Knit and Purl Stitch Version (Using Garter and Reverse Stockinette Textures for Different Sections)

Mikae Toma

This pouch was not made to hold a particular object.

The color considerations are quite similar to the first design. The darker color is again used for the main body of the pouch, and the lighter color is used for the flap, with a transitional section in between.

For this pouch, I played with knit and purl stitches to create both garter and reverse stockinette textures. It is exciting to work consciously with these different stitches and to observe the different quality of the texture as well as the different tensions and other effects they have on the knitting. Observing the stitches and their effects on the fabric is an important aspect of the process.

Again, I began knitting at the top front of the pouch. I knitted some rows with garter stitch and then switched to reverse stockinette toward the bottom part of the pouch.

To create the reverse stockinette texture, I alternated purl with knit rows. I introduced the change gradually, in a dynamic way. First, I introduced 1 row of knit only and then a little later 2 rows and then switched to an all-knit texture. The purl side of the fabric would become the outside of the pouch (reverse stockinette).

One can observe how the texture changes as the piece grows. The reverse stockinette fabric is smoother and flatter, and also less flexible than the garter stitch section, which consists of rows of horizontal wave-like lines, loosely placed next to each other. When garter stitch is stretched, rows of knit stitches become visible between those lines. This makes it relatively loose and flexible, but well-balanced, and visually it has an expansive quality. Looking at the reverse stockinette texture, the surface is again made up of wave-like horizontal lines, but here they are much more densely packed. On the knit side, the stockinette texture is very smooth and even, quite different from the other side.

When my piece had reached the right length, which I again determined by folding it up, I switched to garter stitch for a short section of the upper back and also changed to the lighter color. To support the opening and closing movements of the flap, I created a short reverse stockinette band within the garter stitch section.

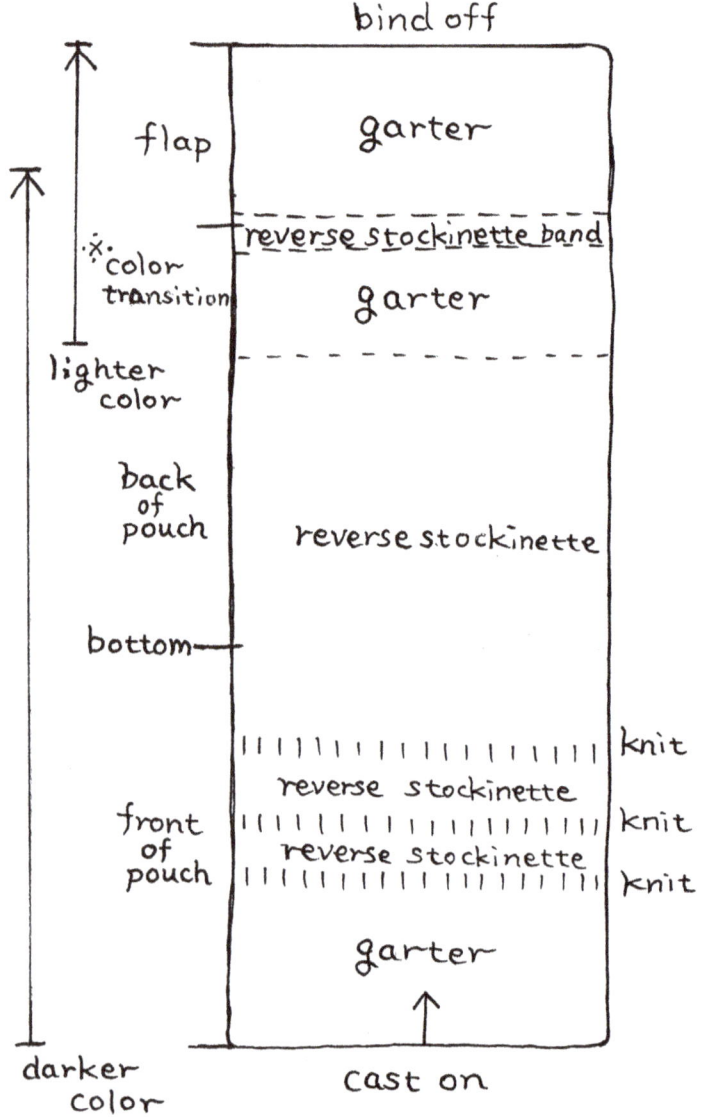

DIAGRAM 1. At color transitions: alternate lighter and darker colors every two rows. Changing colors always happens on the right side of the piece, which will become the outside of the pouch.

For the flap, I continued knitting the full width of the garter stitch section, making sure that it would be long enough to securely hold the object placed inside (with the help of two buttons added after sewing up the sides). I created the loops for the buttons by making tight chain stitches with a crochet hook and tried to space them in a balanced way. Between the loops, I wove in and secured the yarn somewhat under the bound-off edge, so that the loops seem to grow out organically from the piece and are short and almost hidden. After the sides were sewn together and the buttons added, the piece was ready to serve its purpose and looked quite beautiful.

Designing and Making Your Own Pouch

After making pouches by working through the above descriptions, try making your own designs. Choose your yarn and try making a pouch. Work with at least two colors so that you can play with the color transition from the bottom to the top and flap of the pouch (if it's intended to hold a particular object, think about what colors would be most suitable). Try out different stitch patterns and notice how they change the fabric of your pouch. This experience will serve you well when you move on to larger designs.

Many different variations of small pouches

Part Two: The Knitting Journey

Recommended Ways of Working

As you begin to contemplate making a piece of clothing, it is good to reflect upon the universal aspects of the physical body and its basic structure—and, of course, you have to picture the unique characteristics of the person for whom you are making this piece. Other considerations are related to practicalities such as the seasons or occasions for which you expect this piece to be worn.

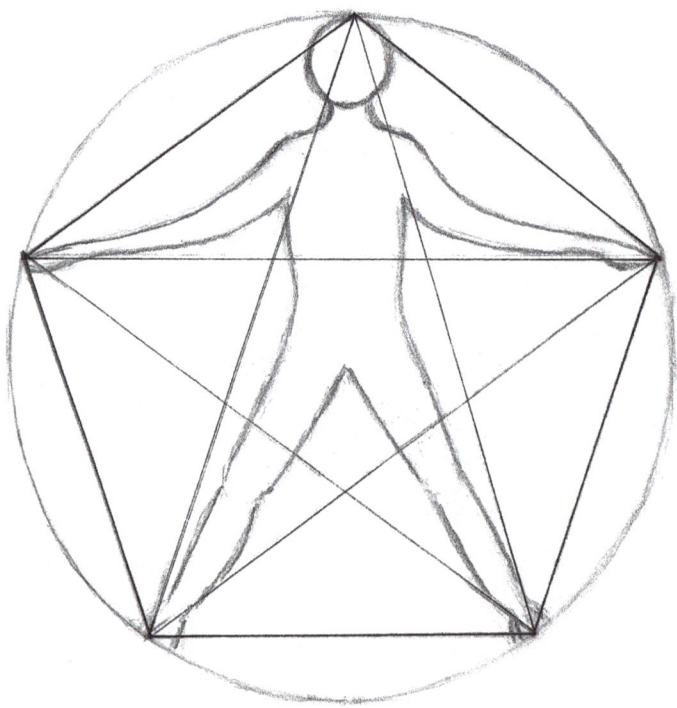

Universal Aspects of the Physical Body

An important characteristic of the human being is uprightness. This uprightness, which is connected to the forces of the ego, allows us to stand between heaven and earth, with the darkness of the earth beneath our feet and the realms of light above us. Our physical body has a clearly defined vertical center, which is strongly marked by the spine, and it has a left and a right side. These two sides are almost symmetrical, while the front and back of the body are very different from each other. Thanks to our limbs, our arms and legs, we have the possibility to move and be active in the world.

The physical body has evolved over eons of time and is filled with great wisdom. When we move our feet shoulder-width apart and raise our outstretched arms, the bodily form fits into a circle, marks the points of a pentagon, and delineates a star, a pentagram form. It also fits into a square, with the legs placed closely together and the arms stretched out horizontally. The golden ratio, an ideal measure of proportion, prevails throughout, and a harmonious blend of function and beauty can be detected in the entire organism, with the metamorphosis of forms as underlying principle. The whole organism is not a closed-off entity, but breathes with the surrounding air and the whole cosmos, and it is permeated by the forces of life.

Unique Aspects of the Individual

The physical body harbors the individuality, the soul and spirit nature, of a human being. This nature, although less tangible and perpetually evolving, can be experienced in many different ways. One's physiognomy, facial expressions, voice, temperament, and the quality of gestures and deeds all bear an individual stamp. Other aspects to consider are the gender and age of a person, the shape and size of the body, and the skin, hair, and eye colors.

Practical Considerations

As mentioned above, it is also important to consider:

- The seasons of the year: Will the piece be worn in spring, summer, fall, or winter?
- The occasion for which a piece is intended: Will it be worn on festive occasions or at work?
- The combination with other pieces in the wardrobe is another area to look into: How will it blend with other pieces?

The Process of Creation

We recommend that you always work with an emphasis on the process of creation, with a kind of listening gesture, rather than primarily focusing on the end result. When you are truly present in the moment and immersed in the process, your intentions may take on the quality of love for the task at hand. This loving attention is bound to open doors to intuitive ways of working; the yarns in your hands, the colors, the stitches, shapes, and textures will begin to speak and reveal their qualities, their inner nature—and you will be able to connect more deeply with your creative self.

Phases of the Process

The process of creation encompasses distinct and sometimes overlapping phases, although, of course, each human being gives each phase a unique character.

- First, an *idea* may light up in your mind. This idea may be based on one of the knitting guidelines in this book, or it may be an inspiration you have received while working on another piece. There are, of course, many possibilities.
- Then you go through an exploratory phase of *reflecting on* and *warming up* to this idea. In this phase, sketching the basic form as well as transitions from dark to light colors will be helpful. Choosing yarns and knitting needles and making swatches are other important steps.

- This preparatory work will help you to become really engaged in a concrete way. It may spark new ideas or ways of working, or it may simply confirm that you are on the right track and that you are ready to begin knitting the actual piece.
- In the next phase, you will become active in many different ways. From the gathering of the materials and tools to the actual knitting, you will be engaged in *movements* of an inner and outer nature to slowly bring *form*.
- Your devoted, wakeful activity and loving attention will lead to good results and enhance your artistic way of knowing.

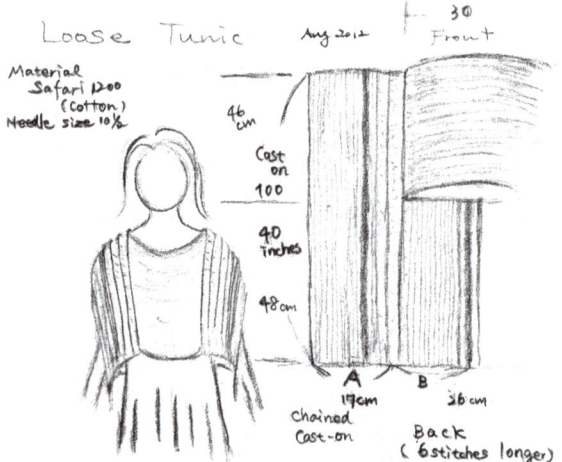

From the beginning to the end of the process, you need to carry a realistic picture of the piece of clothing you would like to make, and you need to know where on the body you are knitting. This becomes clear when you try on the piece or hold it up against your body. This can be done even in the early stages of the process. Remember: The body is your pattern, and the beauty of nature's evolving shapes and colors can be your inspiration.

Note-taking throughout the process and a review at the end are helpful practices.

As you progress with your work, keep trying on your evolving piece. You want to be sure that it will fit well in the end and will have the look you are aiming for. When you are pleased with what you see, you will be encouraged to proceed. Sometimes you will discover the need to redo what you have done, or you will need to pull out several rows. You should consider these corrective measures as an integral part of the process and never see them as a kind of punishment or failure on your part. Redoing some of the work gives you new opportunities, and you will learn something important along the way.

After the knitting is done and the yarn ends woven in, your piece might need some final touches, like blocking to even out the stitches and adjust the final form (see "On Blocking and Caring for Your Woolen Knits," page 150 in the appendix). Then comes the moment of wearing it and combining it with other pieces in the wardrobe. What a special moment it is! It can be filled with joy and a sense of accomplishment.

When you have completed your piece, you have progressed in your knitting journey, and you are in possession of something truly special: a gift from nature transformed by your hands and spiritual striving into a beautiful, functional, and health-giving garment.
You might also sense that you have been engaged in important acts of courage and self-transformation.

Making Swatches

Always make swatches with the yarns, knitting needles, and type of stitches you intend to use for a project. You will learn not only what your knitting will look and feel like, but you will also be able to find the knitting gauge, the number of stitches per inch. This is important information if you intend to follow a pattern and duplicate the knitting gauge indicated. It is also important information for creating your own design or a larger version of an existing design.

For most of the designs in this book, we recommend knitting a square of approximately four inches. You can follow the gauge indications on your yarn label to get an approximate indication of the number of stitches to cast on. You can also use our gauge indication as a basis. If the design is knitted in stockinette texture (knit stitches on one side of the fabric and purl stitches on the other), make the swatch in stockinette as well and add an additional garter stitch border of two garter ridges (four knit rows) each at the bottom and top, and two stitches on each of the two sides, so that the swatch lies relatively flat. When finished, you may want to steam it lightly with an iron so it lies flat. Then put it on a flat surface and, using a ruler or commercially available stitch gauge, count the number of stitches in at least two inches of the knitting. Divide the number by two to get the number of stitches per inch.

If you are aiming for a particular gauge and have not yet achieved it, switch to smaller or larger needles, as needed, and make another swatch. Continue "swatching" until you achieve the desired gauge.

The proper "swatch" to gauge a piece knitted in the round is a small piece, perhaps the size of a headband. See the instructions for knitting headbands, starting on page 149.

For the designs that are knitted in the round or are based on flat pieces, knitted in horizontal fashion, it is not critical to know the number of rows per inch—which can also be counted in the swatch—since the length of the knitting can be determined by trying on the evolving piece to suit your taste.

For the designs that are based on flat pieces knitted vertically, the length of the pieces is determined by the number of stitches.

There are metal stitch gauges available that facilitate measuring gauge by providing a narrow corner window of two inches in length in both directions. They also feature a diagonal row of holes that allow for easy measuring of knitting needle sizes.

Adjusting Sizes

Instructions are given for creating the garment shown in the photo, as closely as possible. Your garments, however, will be unique. As you work through the projects, we hope that you will become more confident in making changes to adapt them to your own body or those you are knitting for. You may also need to make adjustments for knitting with different yarns and in a different gauge than given in the instructions.

The following are general instructions that can be referred to for all projects. Some of the projects include more specific advice for various points where calculations need to be made.

After you make a gauge swatch with the yarn and needle size you wish to use, you can determine the number of stitches to cast on by measuring at the place where the beginning edge of the garment will fall. Multiply your gauge count by the number of inches desired. For example, if you want a piece to measure 20 inches and have a gauge of 2.5 stitches per inch, you will cast on 50 stitches.

Where the garment is shaped by changing needle sizes, follow the same principle, as well as changing to a needle one or two sizes smaller or larger, as indicated in the instructions.

As you knit horizontally, length can be adjusted by knitting more or fewer rows or rounds. Holding up or trying on the garment will help you determine this length. To try on an unfinished garment made on a circular needle, you may need to put the stitches on a string or on a longer circular needle temporarily. Putting the stitches on the wire parts of two circular needles also works quite well.

When knitting vertically across the body, as mentioned above, the number of stitches determines the garment length. It is therefore critical to take good measurements of the body and to take into account the number of stitches per inch from the gauge swatch.

As you become more familiar with the elements of garment construction, you will be freed from needing to follow patterns exactly, and be able to create your own variations. You will truly be knitting by heart, an active process of creation.

THE PROJECTS

PART TWO: THE KNITTING JOURNEY

Spiral Gestures: Knitting in the Round

We find spiral gestures everywhere in nature, where they fill us with awe and wonder.

The perfect spiral of the nautilus shell or the intricate patterns of the pine cone come immediately to mind, and if we take the time to observe a plant, we may find leaves spiraling up the stem toward the blossom. On the crown of our head, we human beings are marked by a spiral formed by our hair, and scientific research has revealed the spiral structure of our DNA and the spiral gestures of our galaxy as seen from space. No wonder that in times gone by, the mystic symbol of the spiral was carved into stone, painted on walls, etched into metal, and tattooed onto human bodies.

When we knit in the round, we quickly become relaxed and centered, as we are engaged in forming a spiral with our yarn, using the tools of our knitting needles. The process of knitting in the round is continuous, with no need to end and begin a row. The spiraling comes to an end only when the project is finished. When we create a capelet, top, or sweater in this way, the completed garment spirals around our body, forming a kind of cocoon. We can spiral from the top down, starting at the neck and shoulders, or we can spiral from the bottom up, starting around the hips or the waist. There is even the possibility of knitting in both directions within the same piece.

By knitting in the round, we create three-dimensional sculptural pieces in an organic way. There is no need to sew separate pieces together. As these sculptural garments develop and grow, they can be tried on again and again. In this way, we can make sure that the pieces will fit us perfectly.

For smaller projects like mittens or socks we use four or five double-pointed needles; for larger items we use a circular needle. These come in various lengths to suit each project.

The knitting direction, which is either from the top down or the bottom up, allows for a design that emphasizes a progression from dark to light in color and from heaviness to lightness in texture from the bottom to the top of the garment. In this way we can artistically express how we are placed on Earth in connection with the whole cosmos. We can also keep in mind the inner light and warmth radiating from the face and maybe even the hands, by embellishing the yoke and the sleeves of a top or a sweater. Of course, with the choice of color, we can express many other subtle aspects connected with the inner nature of the person for whom the garment is made.

Introductory Project: Headbands

Renate Hiller

Headbands are wonderful, small projects to explore knitting in the round. Using a short circular needle and various types of yarns in a variety of colors will allow you to explore the techniques needed for this section.

The headband is a good-sized project to serve as a swatch in order to establish the gauge of a larger piece that will be knitted in the round, as noted in "Making Swatches," page 46.

With the help of several knitted examples, we will guide you as you explore the use of:

- various fibers and textures
- knit and purl stitches and their practical and visual impact on your knitting
- color gestures, color combinations, and transitions

We recommend that you create several headbands before you make any of the other projects featured in this section.

Headbands are extremely practical; they can warm our ears and our foreheads, and—depending on where and how we place them on our head—they can hold our hair in place. Like all accessories, they can enhance our looks and be truly beautiful as well, especially if they are paired with wrist warmers, mittens, scarves, or cowls with similar design motifs. And they are perfect small projects to make use of yarn remnants collected over the years.

Headband Design 1

Materials & Tools

Yarn: 1 oz, about 70 yds, of single-ply spindle-spun yarn, fine- to worsted-weight

Needles: Circular knitting needle, size 10 (or size needed to obtain gauge), 16 in. long

Gauge: 4 1/2 sts per inch in purl (reverse stockinette) sections

Color: At least three shades, graded from dark to light

I used: Naturally colored Jacob sheep's wool in shades of ivory and gray.

I fell in love with this small accessory when I knitted it with spindle-spun Jacob sheep's wool during a one-year Sheep to Shawl course at the Fiber Craft Studio. I sometimes wear it together with a gray alpaca sweater and at other times with a triangular shawl made from hand-spun yarn that has a similar quality (although it came from a Border Leicester sheep).

The colors move from ivory to dark gray, like a shaded drawing, in the first band, which is meant to be worn close to the face. In the second, somewhat wider band, this color progression is repeated in a slightly darker version.

The headband I made is soft and light, like a cloud, and brings such subtle warmth that it feels like a blessing to wear it. I not only wear it as a headband, but also as a neck warmer, twisting it around itself. It reminds me of the herd of Jacob sheep we frequently visited at Jenny Jump Farm that had their home at the foot of a mountain in a lovely area in northern New Jersey, and of the kindness of farmer Joany, who let us pick one of her softest, most beautiful fleeces for our course. The fleece we picked came from a sweet ewe named Felicity, and had an overall tone of ivory with patches of dark to light shades of gray.

Jacob sheep

During our course, all participants were able to choose locks of the fleece and spin yarns with a spindle ranging from ivory to dark gray and many shades of gray in between. We used our first small skeins of one-ply yarn for knitting headbands. We soaked the skeins in warm water and hung them up to dry, with a light weight attached to the bottom of each one to set the twist.

Here are indications for my headband, which, a few years after its creation, has become a kind of archetype for me. This headband has the same width all around. I designed it in such a way that it can be easily gathered at the back of the head into a narrow band, while it fully covers the forehead and the ears. To facilitate this flexibility, I knitted two purl sections separated by a narrower knit section. The two "purl" sections look like concave bands that are visually separated by the "knit" section.

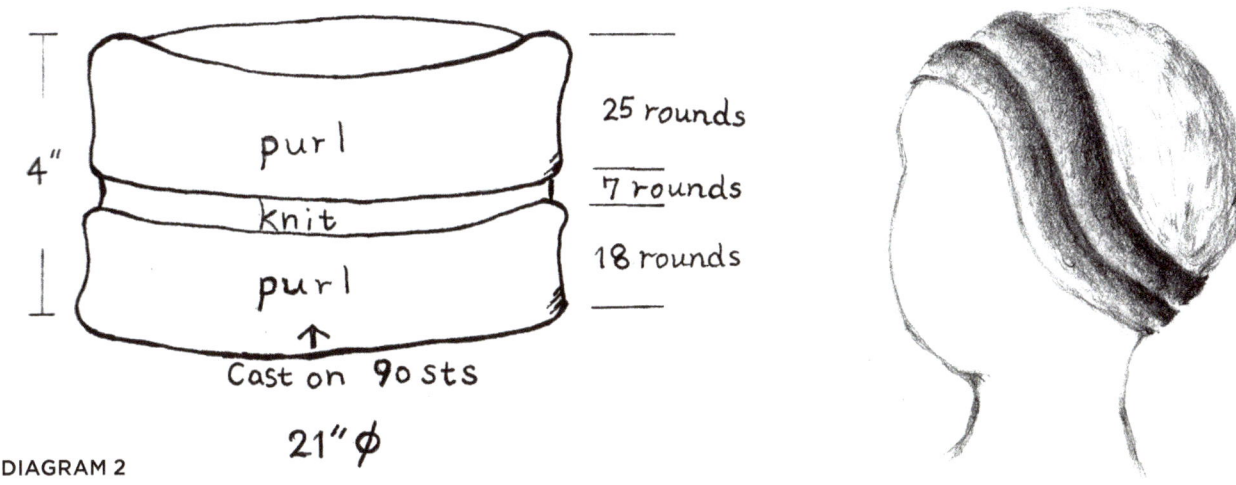

DIAGRAM 2

Instructions:

Cast on 90 stitches on the circular needle, using the yarn in the lightest shade of color (in the sample, light gray).

Join for working in the round, being careful not to twist the chain of stitches on the needle. Purl every round.

After several rounds, when your piece measures an inch or so, you can switch to the medium gray yarn, and after several more, to dark gray yarn. Purl 18 rounds total for the first purl band.

Switch to light gray yarn and knit 7 rounds.

Continuing with light gray yarn, begin the second purl band. Again, switch colors from light to medium to dark after each set of several rounds to produce a graded effect. Try knitting fewer rounds with light gray this time, so that this purl band is darker overall than the first one.

Purl 25 rounds total. Bind off all stitches.

Headband Design 1 Variation

Inspired by the headband described above, I created this band using a very special cotton yarn that has a hand-spun quality and is organically grown. The dimensions for this band

Materials & Tools

Yarn: 5/8 oz, about 50 yds, of fine- to worsted-weight organic cotton yarn of hand-spun quality

Needles: Circular knitting needle, size 10 (or size needed to obtain gauge), 16 in. long

Gauge: 4 sts per inch in purl (reverse stockinette) sections

Color: Two colors, one dark and one light

I used: Beige and blue colors. The beige was dyed with black walnut hulls and the blues with indigo.

are very close to the one described above. However, it is made up of three bands with two narrow knit (stockinette stitch) sections in between. The first wide band lies flat, close to the face, since it is a garter stitch (knit 1 row, purl 1 row) section, and the two subsequent purl (reverse stockinette) bands have a somewhat convex quality.

The colors transition from light beige at the face to blue toward the top. The blue increases as the beige decreases in an organic way. I used beige only in the first band; the second band begins with two beige rows and then moves to blue only; and the third band begins with one beige row and moves to blue only. The two concave knit sections are worked in blue.

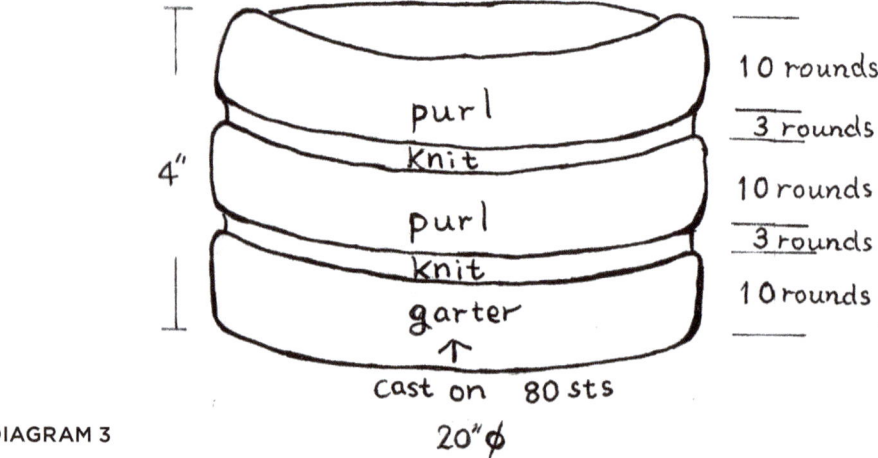

DIAGRAM 3

Instructions:

Cast on 80 stitches, using lighter colored yarn on a circular needle. Join for working in the round, being careful not to twist the first round of stitches.
Knit the first round, purl the second round. Repeat these two rounds 4 more times, for 10 rounds total (garter stitch band).
Knit three rounds.
Begin first purl band: Purl two rounds using lighter color yarn, then switch to darker color yarn and purl 8 more rounds—10 rounds total.
Knit three rounds.
Begin second purl band. Switch to lighter colored yarn. Purl one round. Switch to darker color yarn and purl 9 more rounds—10 rounds total.
Bind off all stitches.
You may wish to experiment with different ways of grading the colors, using two or even three colors.

Headband Design 2

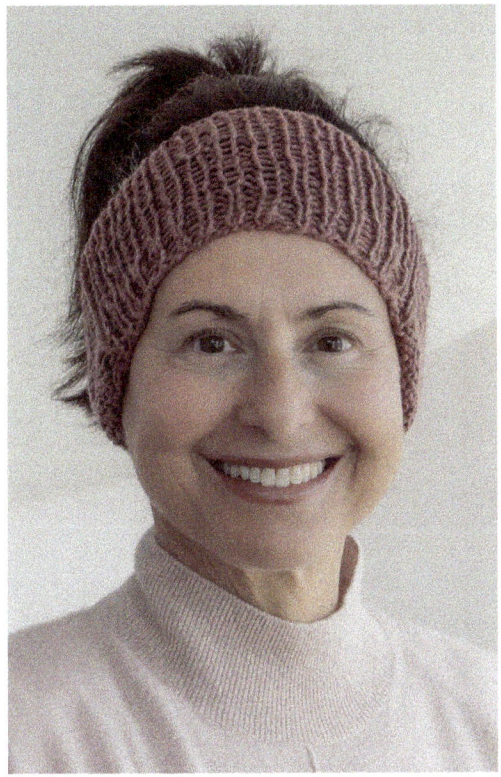

Materials & Tools

Yarn: 5/8 oz, about 40 yds, worsted-weight wool/alpaca yarn

Needles: Circular knitting needle, size 10 (or size needed to obtain gauge), 16 in. long

Gauge: 4 sts per inch in purl (reverse stockinette) section

Color: Choose any color you find suitable for a headband

I used: A beautiful rosy red. The color arose after a dye bath in brazilwood and a short immersion in a black walnut bath.

For this design, I used a worsted-weight wool/alpaca yarn, a remnant from the Seamless Sweater on page 78. This yarn, when knitted with the same-sized knitting needle as Headband Design 1, creates a denser, firmer texture, and the band fits more tightly around my head.

As you can see from the photos and the drawings, the design is quite different from Design 1, in keeping with the different type of yarn. When I thought about introducing ribbing to the bands to bring elasticity in the circumference, it became clear to me that I did not want to use ribbing all around. This would stiffen the bands somewhat, so that they could not be gathered together comfortably behind the neck. In a moment of inspiration, I decided to introduce ribbing over the front part of the band, and toward the back to make use of the dynamic quality of the rolled edges created by pure knit or pure purl sections. I decided to use an all-purl section (reverse stockinette) that would also cover the ears at the transition from the ribbing to the purling.

As I was executing and finishing the piece, I was very pleased to see how beautiful and functional it turned out to be. I especially like the organic look of the partial curling at the transition from the ribbing to the purling on both sides, which forms just the right spaces for the ears.

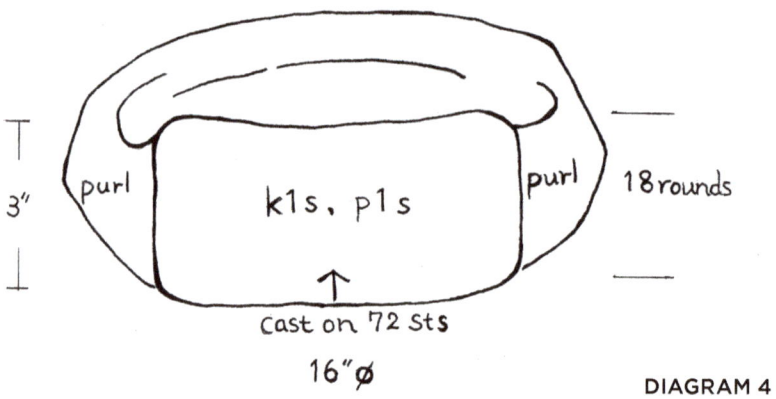

DIAGRAM 4

Instructions:

Cast on 72 stitches using a circular needle. Join for knitting in the round, being careful not to twist the first row of stitches on the needle.

Work k1, p1, 16 times for the ribbing section (32 stitches). Purl 40 stitches.

Repeat this round for a total of 18 rounds. Bind off all stitches.

Headband Design 2 Variation

Materials & Tools

Yarn: 3/4 oz, about 45 yds worsted-weight wool/alpaca yarn

Needles: Circular knitting needle, size 10 (or size needed to obtain gauge), 16 in. long

Gauge: 4 sts per inch in purl (reverse stockinette) band

Color: Any color you deem suitable for a headband

I used: A lovely blue. The color arose after a dye bath in indigo, and another short bath in a black walnut pot.

This version is very similar to the above design. I used the same type of yarn in a different color. However, the ribbing is somewhat wider—ending just before the ears—and the curling section forms one convex band in the center that is framed on both sides by narrow curling edges.

PART TWO: THE KNITTING JOURNEY

Instructions:

Cast on 72 stitches using a circular needle. Join for knitting in the round, being careful not to twist the first row of stitches on the needle.

*Work k1, p1, 20 times to begin the ribbing section (40 stitches). Knit 32 stitches.

Repeat from * 5 times for a total of 6 rounds.

For the next 8 rounds, work k1, p1, 20 times to continue the ribbing section, then purl 32 stitches.

For the next 4 rounds, work k1, p1, 20 times to continue the ribbing section, then knit 32 stitches.

To create a special border at the top of the ribbing section, on the final round change the rhythm of k1, p1 to p1, k1. Work p1, k1 20 times, then knit 32 stitches.

Bind off all stitches.

SPIRAL GESTURES: KNITTING IN THE ROUND

Exploring further

As you make your own headbands, feel free to experiment with yarn type, texture, and color. You may not be able to find close matches to the yarns I used; that's fine! Use what you have and notice how the qualities of the yarn affect your finished project. What are the different benefits of a light, airy yarn, or a thick, dense one? Why does it seem to be more satisfying to place lighter colors near the face? What inclines you to use warmer colors, or cooler colors? What impression do naturally colored or plant-dyed yarns make on you, compared to chemically dyed textiles?

When working with two or more colors, try to sense where to change colors to create a pleasing gradation.

Sample headbands are sized for an average female head. Size adjustments can be made for larger or smaller heads. Just add or subtract the correct number of stitches, according to gauge, for the desired inches of circumference.

The principles you learn through these explorations will be extended and applied to larger garments in the following projects, where you can similarly adapt the examples given by using different yarns and colors.

From Capelet to Sweater

SPIRAL GESTURES: FROM CAPELET TO SWEATER

Capelet
Renate Hiller

Materials & Tools

Yarn: 4 oz, about 250 yds, worsted-weight wool/alpaca and wool/mohair yarns; 2 oz, about 150 yds, silk/wool and mohair bouclé yarns

Needles: Circular knitting needles, sizes 11, 10, and 8, 29 in. long

Gauge: With largest needle, 3 sts per inch

Color: Various shades of two colors that will blend harmoniously

I used: Golden and bluish tones dyed with indigo and onion skins.

This capelet is knitted in the round, starting at the bottom. It adds a festive note to any simple dress or top and brings warmth to the shoulder and neck area. It can be worn in different ways: in a draped or more smooth fashion, and with the knit or purl side facing outward.

I created this capelet while I was vacationing at the seaside. I had taken along a basket of small- and medium-sized skeins of smooth wool and mohair and silk bouclé yarns from the supplies of the Fiber Craft Studio, unsure of what I would end up making. I had chosen yarns in cool blues and golden tones, aware that the blues would go well with the color of my eyes and probably already fantasizing about the colors of sand and sea. A few days later, while sitting on the terrace after a wonderful swim, basket in hand, playing with my treasure—feeling the textures and observing the colors—the idea of a capelet was born.

Since I wanted to take up knitting in the round with large circular needles, this was the right project to begin. I had previously knitted mittens, socks, and hats in the round using four double-pointed needles, slowly learning how to handle four needles, how to make a properly integrated thumb, turn a heel, and bring a hat to a harmonious closure. These are no easy tasks, since mittens, socks, and hats need to fit perfectly.

The capelet, on the other hand, was easy to make with a circular needle, and I enjoyed the even, continuous flow that the simplicity of the project provided. Starting the knitting at the bottom (more or less above the elbows), I was curious to see where the colors and textures would lead me, imagining always the area of the body that would be covered by the fabric I was creating, and also trying on the piece quite frequently. I was able to play with the colors and textures in subtle ways, thanks to the mohair and silk bouclé, the variation of fibers and shades of color in each skein, and the small skeins that I was using. I began with heavier-looking yarns (silk bouclé) and darker colors with a bit of lightness shining through at the bottom, followed by the lighter tones of the wool and mohair bouclé yarns in the chest area. To express the firmness and strength of the shoulders, I used somewhat darker tones, which then transitioned to lighter colors and worsted-weight yarns toward the top, close to the neck and face. Throughout the piece there is a shining quality that intensifies towards the face.

I had first intended to wear the piece with the knit (stockinette) side facing outward, but while working on it and trying it on I found that the color transitions were more beautiful and more subtle on the purl (reverse stockinette) side. I also liked the horizontal flow of the purl stitches better. With this side facing outward, the top edge curls toward the inside, which frames the neckline and face beautifully.

Rather than decreasing the number of stitches to shape the piece, I used knitting needles in different sizes: a size 11 needle at the bottom, followed by sizes 10 and 8. This not only shaped the piece but made the stitches bigger and looser toward the bottom and smaller and tighter toward the top, which was in keeping with the whole design.

For this piece, I aligned all yarn changes in the center back and wove in the ends on the knit side, which I had decided would be the inside of the garment.

The capelet is an ideal piece for using up remnants and making them shine.

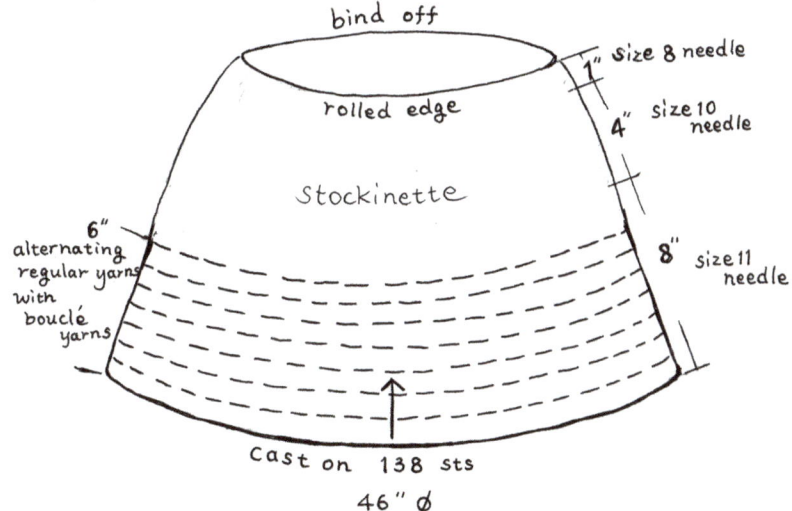

DIAGRAM 5

Instructions:
Make a swatch with the yarns, knitting needles, and stitches indicated. If necessary, adjust the needle sizes to obtain proper gauge (see "Making Swatches," page 45, and "Adjusting Sizes," page 47).
Cast on 138 stitches, using worsted-weight yarn in the darkest shade and largest size circular needle.

Join for working in the round, being careful not to twist the first row of stitches on the needle.

Knit every round, alternating regular and bouclé yarns, until the piece measures 6 inches in length. Continue knitting with regular yarns only until the piece measures 8 inches in length.

Switch to the medium-sized needle and knit with regular yarn in medium dark shades for 4 more inches; 12 inches total length.

Switch to the smallest needle and knit for one more inch using the lightest shades; 13 inches total length.

Bind off all stitches.

Try on the piece as it evolves, so you know where on the body you are knitting.

The capelet can be worn with either the knit side or the purl side of the fabric facing outward. Weave in yarn ends on the side you wish to be the inside.

Size Adjustment

For knitting in a different gauge or in smaller or larger sizes, see general instructions for adjusting sizes on page 47.

Capelet Variation 1

This variation, modeled by our friend Janet, was created by our friend Sono. For this project, Sono dug into her treasure trove of plant-dyed yarns and came up with a symphony of red and orange tones, interspersed with some gentle greens. The mohair bouclé, with its luster, enhances the rich tones of the wool/alpaca yarns. Like the original design, the whole piece was knitted in stockinette texture.

When we compare the original design and this variation, the importance of the language of color becomes apparent. The blue and golden tones of the original speak softly and are somewhat cool in nature, while the reds and oranges speak more loudly and convey a sense of warmth.

Capelet Variation 2
Renate Hiller

This variation is modeled by our friend Sono. For this capelet I used smooth, worsted-weight yarn, a combination of wool and mohair, as well as mohair bouclé yarn. I created purl bands (reverse stockinette) of varying widths that are separated by single rounds of knit stitches, worked in the textured bouclé. The yarn ends left from changing colors and yarn types are not woven in, but are knotted together and hang down freely in the center front of the piece.

It was, above all, Japanese indigo that I had grown in the garden that inspired me to make this variation on the capelet design. I was captivated by the process of kneading the fresh

leaves together with small skeins of yarn and seeing the colors emerge under my hands: gentle blues and turquoises of exquisite beauty! The strong yarns (wool blended with mohair) I had chosen withstood the kneading very well and gave the knitted piece a beautiful sculptural quality. I partnered the indigo colors with tans from fresh black walnut hulls, since the nuts were just falling off the trees all around my neighborhood at the time. What a beautiful combination this is—the result of a close collaboration with nature at the end of summer and the beginning of fall.

Capelet Variation 3

Mikae Toma

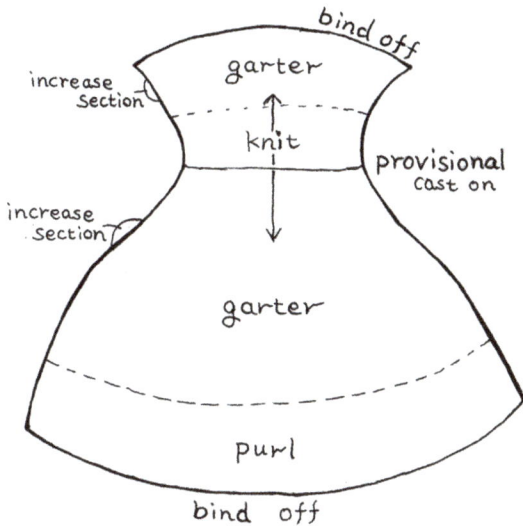

DIAGRAM 6

I shaped this capelet by increasing and decreasing stitches rather than by using different sized knitting needles. The knitting is a bit more complicated than the previous projects, as it is worked in two directions. It starts at the neckline with a provisional cast-on (see "Techniques" in the appendix on page 149) and is first worked downward. After binding off the bottom edge, the stitches are picked up from the provisional cast-on edge and worked upward to the top edge, creating the collar. The folded collar not only looks lovely, but also brings extra warmth to the neckline.

The yarn I used is a hand-spun single-ply wool from a Jacob fleece. The natural colors of gray, brown, and white were sorted into lighter and darker shades and dyed with several local plants. The colors were alternated and blended to create a gradation from darker colors at the bottom to lighter colors at the top.

Circular Cowl

Mikae Toma

Materials & Tools

Yarn: 4 oz, about 190 yds, worsted-weight single-ply wool/mohair yarn

Needles: Circular knitting needles, size 10, 16 and 29 in. long

Gauge: 3 sts per inch in reverse stockinette

Color: A single color with subtle variations of shading

I used: Shades of rusty, blue-greenish brown, created with indigo and black walnut.

This circular cowl is knitted in the round, using bands consisting of several rows of purl stitches (reverse stockinette) followed by one round of knit stitches to create a ripple effect.

As with Capelet Variation 3, knitting is started at the neckline with the provisional cast-on method (see "Techniques" on page 149 in the appendix), knitted downward to the bottom edge, and then a collar is added by knitting from the provisional cast-on upward to the top edge. The cowl can be worn over a jacket or other piece of clothing in a loose fashion, or it can be stretched over the shoulders.

The idea for this piece arose from the need to add an extra-warm layer around the neck and shoulder area of a particular dark silver-gray jacket. It was an interesting process to come to this design, which is related to the neck and shoulder area of the Circular Top (page 69). Since I had already explored a kind of ripple effect (although less pronounced) for that design, this little cowl was born fairly fast. It was one of those pieces that I did not need to struggle with at all.

Purl rounds tend to come forward, in contrast with knit rounds. They create a more convex gesture, giving an impression of fullness. This becomes more apparent when knit rounds appear here and there between the purl rounds. Be sure to observe the reverse side of the knitting, where you will see the opposite texture, with the single rounds of purl stitches (knit rounds in the front) popping out from the overall knit background.

For this cowl I used a single-ply yarn with a loosely twisted quality, which enhances the fullness of the convex sections. As the piece progresses toward the bottom, the size of each ripple (purl band) gets larger in width and number of stitches, due to the increases made in the knit rounds. The bottom ripple needs to be made especially wide—more than the organic progression would call for—due to the inward rolling effect that happens naturally with several purl rounds. At the top edge, I have chosen to create an outwardly rolled edge (made with several knit rounds) in order to express openness close to the face.

I recommend that you create the ripples of your piece by observing the shape of your own neck-and-shoulder area, rather than having a strictly regulated rhythm. An interesting variation of this piece could be made by inserting two knit rounds rather than one in between the purl bands.

The ripple effect brings a very peaceful yet active feeling to the face and echoes the roundness of the entire head and curved line of the chin. It allows the cowl to sit well on the shoulders and to move freely with the movements of the shoulders and upper arms. The cowl can also bring a soft quality to the neckline of a jacket.

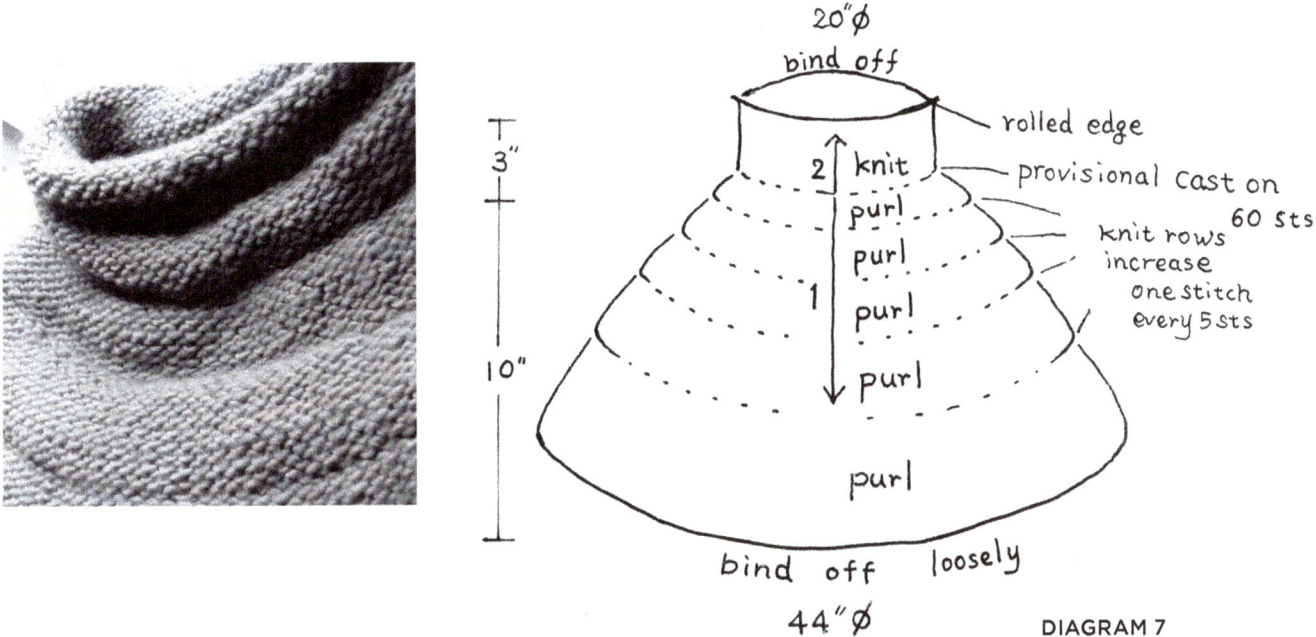

DIAGRAM 7

Instructions:
Make a swatch with the yarns, knitting needles, and stitches indicated. If necessary, adjust the needle sizes to obtain proper gauge (see "Making Swatches," page 45, and "Adjusting Sizes," page 47). Using a provisional cast-on technique, cast on 60 stitches on the 16-inch circular needle. Join for working in the round, being careful not to twist the first row of stitches on the needle.
Purl 7 rounds.
On the next round, knit 5 stitches, M1 (single increase). Repeat to end of round.
As you continue to increase the number of stitches over the next several rows, you will eventually get to the point where the stitches no longer fit on the 16-inch needle, and you will need to change to the 29-inch needle.
Purl 8 rounds.
On the next round, knit 6 stitches, M1, repeat to end of round.
Purl 9 rounds.
On the next round, knit 7 stitches, M1, repeat to end of round.
Purl 11 rounds.
On the next round, knit 8 stitches, M1, repeat to end of round.
Purl 18 rounds. Bind off all stitches loosely.
Pick up stitches from the provisional cast-on edge, using the 16-inch circular needle.
Knit all rounds until this section measures 3 inches. Bind off all stitches loosely.

Size Adjustment
For knitting in a different gauge or in smaller or larger sizes, see general instructions for adjusting sizes in "Recommended Ways of Working."
Depending on the stitch count, you may need to adjust the number of increases in the knit rounds and the number of rounds between increases. In the sample garment, there are 12 stitches added in each increase round. To make your cowl grow wider more quickly, insert more increases. To keep it narrower for longer, insert fewer increases.

Circular Cowl Variation
Mikae Toma

This cowl is almost the same as the basic design featured on page 66. However, in this variation, the ripple effect is slightly more pronounced, with two rounds of knit stitches between the purl sections. In addition, a gradation of dark to light shades progresses organically, as the dark shades, prevalent toward the bottom, decrease, and the light shades increase. A worsted-weight merino yarn, dyed with madder root and an iron mordant, was used.

Circular Top

Mikae Toma

Materials & Tools

Yarn: 9 oz, about 675 yds, worsted-weight 2-ply yarn

Needles: Circular knitting needles, sizes 10 and 8, 29 in. long

Gauge: 3 sts per inch with larger needle

Color: At least two harmonizing colors in darker and lighter shades

I used: Light gray Jacob sheep's wool; for the green tones, I used Osage orange overdyed with indigo; for the earth tones I used cutch and dyer's coreopsis.

The Circular Top is a unique piece; it feels like an extended capelet with holes for the arms. The wavelike steps around the neck create a circular movement, echoing the roundness of the face.

The inspiration for this project began with the quality of the natural heather-gray Jacob wool yarn; its somewhat rustic, almost coarse, earthy look and subtle luster intrigued me. I dyed a few skeins with four different plants to create many gradations in tone. As the piece progressed from the bottom to the top, I chose darker to lighter shades, with greenish tones giving strength to the bottom and chest areas.

Although I spent several weeks contemplating the design of this vest, I began without a clear vision of what the outcome would be. I began knitting at the bottom using mainly the purl stitch (reverse stockinette). This way of knitting would make the grain of the stitches horizontally aligned, which would go well with the way I imagined the color gradations.

Since I was knitting this piece in the round, I thought about the color changes and the subtle, seam-like line that would occur along the center of the back. Since I wanted to create a well-balanced piece, I did not want to make the "seam" on one side of the vest. I kept questioning how it would look and feel to have this seam-line in the back. But it worked quite nicely, and it felt just right.

After living into the quality of the transition between lower and upper torso and expressing it in knitting with colored yarns, I came to a place where I had to do something for the armholes. It was clear to me that the circular flow of knitting would have to continue without interruption. This was made possible by binding off some stitches on both sides at the proper place (after checking this placement on the body) and, with the following round, casting on again. To create enough space for the arms and allow for proper movement, I cast on more stitches than I had bound off.

The section from the armholes to the neck has a very different quality that did not allow me to just continue purling as before. Both the colors and the stitches needed to express the change. This part of the body includes the shoulders and part of the upper arms; therefore, there is more outer movement compared with the inner movement of the lower torso. In addition, the width of the piece has to narrow toward the neck. To express and facilitate the outer movements, I created a kind of ripple effect by inserting two knit rows between several purl rows. The knit rows appeared as grooves in the purl texture, and they were the perfect place to make the necessary decreases without them being visible. In order to differentiate the front of the neckline from the back, I did decrease a few more stitches in the front with the final decrease round, which made the back a bit higher and narrower than the front. It is a very subtle change that makes quite a difference.

Instructions:

Make a swatch with the yarns, knitting needles, and stitches indicated. If necessary, adjust the needle sizes to obtain proper gauge (see "Making Swatches," page 45, and "Adjusting Sizes," page 47).

Cast on 132 stitches using the larger circular needle and darker yarn. Join for working in the round, being careful not to twist the first row of stitches on the needle.

Purl one round, then knit one round (garter stitch for lower edge border).

Purl the next round, then continue purling all rounds, changing colors as desired to create a gradation from dark to light, changing colors at what will become the center back of the garment, until the piece measures 13 inches in length from the bottom cast-on edge.

On the next round, purl 25 stitches, bind off 15, purl 52, bind off 15, and purl 25.

On the next round, purl 25 stitches, cast on 24, purl 52, cast on 24 stitches, and purl 25. 150 stitches total.

Switch to darker yarn again and continue purling all rounds, changing colors as desired to again create a gradation from dark to light, until the piece measures 3 inches from the armhole cast-on edge.

Knit two rounds.

Switch to smaller circular needle. Purl every round, changing colors as desired, until the piece measures 1 1/2 inches from the last knit round.

Knit two rounds.

Purl next round, then continue purling every round, changing colors as desired, until the piece measures 1 inch from the last knit round.

Knit one round.

Begin first decrease round: k2tog, *k2, k2tog, repeat from * to the seamline. You should have 112 stitches remaining.

Purl next round, then continue purling every round, changing colors as desired, until the piece measures 5/8 inch from the last knit round.

Knit one round.

Begin second decrease round: [k2, k2tog] 7 times across the back of the neckline up to the left shoulder.

Then k1, [k1, k2tog] 18 times to shape the front neckline, ending with k1.

Next, [k2tog, k2] 7 times across the right shoulder and back. 80 stitches remaining.

Purl two more rounds and bind off all stitches loosely.

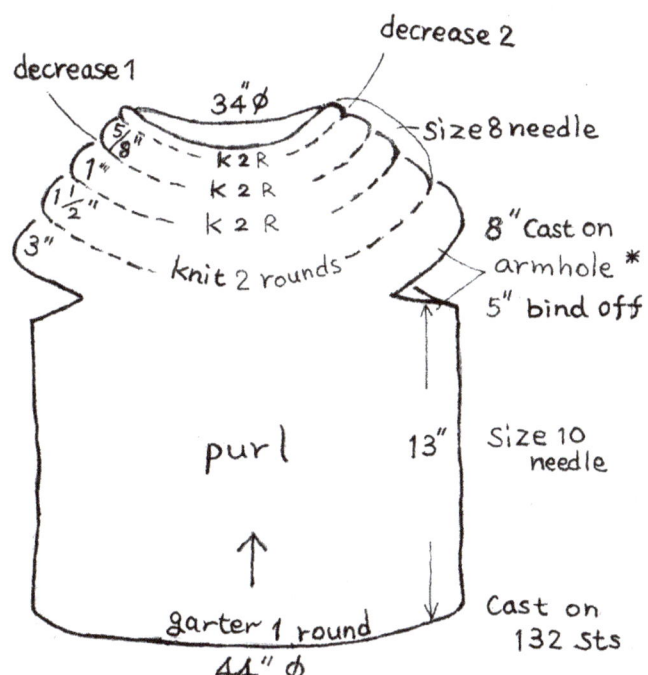

DIAGRAM 8

SPIRAL GESTURES: FROM CAPELET TO SWEATER

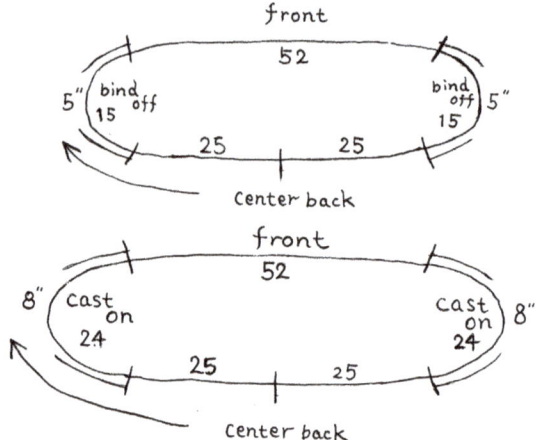

DIAGRAM 9: Armhole creation

Size Adjustment

For knitting in a different gauge or in smaller or larger sizes, see general instructions for adjusting sizes on page 47.

For the Circular Top, you will need to calculate the number of stitches to bind off and cast on at the armholes. For the front and back of the garment, allow an equal number of stitches, each about 40 percent of the total number of stitches. The remaining stitches—about 10 percent on each side —will be bound off to form the armholes. You can "borrow" a stitch or two from the front or back if needed to make the numbers even. In the sample shown, the front has 52 stitches and the back 50. You may write in your own numbers on the diagram or make a copy to work on.

As shown in the diagram above, because you begin each round in the center back, you will first purl half of the back stitches, then bind off the first armhole, then purl all the front stitches, bind off the second armhole, and finally purl the remaining center back stitches.

On the next row, you repeat this process, except that you cast on an additional number of stitches on each side to allow for the wider circumference of the shoulders as well as the movement of the arms. This number should be about 1.6 times the number of stitches that were bound off. (In the example, 15 stitches were bound off, 24 cast on). You may adjust this number for especially wide or narrow shoulders.

The yoke shaping can follow the pattern above, adjusting the number of rounds between knit rounds as needed. Switch to a smaller-sized needle after the first two knit rounds. On the first decrease round, knit the k2, k2tog decrease as many times as it will fit (if it does not come out evenly, it doesn't matter. You might want to add or subtract a decrease).

For the final round of decreases at the neckline, the numbers will need to be adjusted depending on the number of stitches on your needle. Divide your piece into four quadrants: back left, front left, front right, back right. In the back left quadrant, work the k2, k2tog decreases as many times as it will fit. Then work the k1, k2tog decrease across both quadrants of the front. End with the back right quadrant, working the same number of k2, k2tog decreases as you did on the back right.

You can add or subtract a decrease or two from one or another quadrant if needed; for a wider neckline, make fewer decreases; make more for a narrower neck.

Circular Top Variation
Mikae Toma

This top is modeled by our friend Miho. This top was made exactly the same way as the basic Circular Top. The yarn was a single-ply, worsted-weight mohair and wool blend, Lamb's Pride by the Brown Sheep Company, in shades of brown/beige, dyed with cutch (or catechu, an extract made from the wood of a tree in the acacia family). As you can see, using a different type of yarn brings different effects and makes the design unique as well.

Extra-Warm Poncho

Renate Hiller

Materials & Tools

Yarn: 36 oz, about 760 yds, worsted-weight wool/mohair yarn

Needles: Circular knitting needles, size 10, 16 in. long, and size 10 1/2, 29 in. long or longer

Gauge: 3 1/2 sts per inch in stockinette fabric with smaller needle; 3 sts per inch with larger needle

Color: Two harmonizing colors or shades of a single color, one darker main color and one lighter accent color; 4 oz in lighter color, 32 oz in darker color

I used: Medium brown with accents of light beige.

This poncho is modeled by our friend Janet. It is knitted in the round starting at the top, with a two-color design in the cowl that metamorphoses over the yoke area. Although somewhat heavy in weight, it is very pleasant to wear; it combines flexibility with warmth.

In the cowl and in the upper part of the yoke, the distance between the accent ribs becomes wider, and the width of the darker areas increases. In the shoulder area itself, the use of double yarn makes the light-colored accent ribs more pronounced.

I made this piece in preparation for a fall knitting retreat. While designing the piece I was even picturing some of the people that I knew would come.

I wanted to create a cocoon-like piece that would be a perfect companion not only during sunny, cold weather, but also during windy or damp conditions. Jackets and coats made of synthetic materials, although useful in many ways, act as a barrier and shut us off from nature, while garments made of wool allow our body to breathe with its surroundings. While knitting this piece, I often thought of traditional shepherds and their woolen cloaks, which are often felted and tent-like in character and may serve as all-weather shelters for many years.

For extra warmth, I knitted this poncho with a wool/mohair-blend yarn and doubled the yarn beginning in the area of the shoulders (see diagram 10, below). I also created a warm and flexible cowl. In the whole piece, below the shoulder yoke area, narrow bands of two rounds of knitting and two rounds of purling alternate with each other. The knit bands curving toward the inside in a concave way and purl bands toward the outside in a convex way create a flexible double layer that adds extra warmth.

Since I started the piece with the cowl, I set myself the task of creating a dynamic conversation between the brown and light beige colors, with the lighter color starting close to the face and the darker color slowly increasing toward the bottom of the cowl. I felt that the darker color needed to be in the background and the lighter color in the foreground, so I used the brown for the knit bands and the beige for the purl (reverse stockinette) bands. The purl bands became strong accent ribs of light beige, with a truly shining quality, and with a beautiful thin stitch-line of brown in between the beige ribs. (It never ceases to amaze me how beautifully the colors interweave on the purl side of a knitted piece, or when knit and purl rows alternate.) This design then set the tone for the rest of the poncho, and in particular for the yoke.

While the beige purl bands remain a permanent feature, becoming visually more pronounced in the shoulder area through using a double strand of yarn, the brown knit bands change in width. They become wider at the transition from the neck to the shoulders, creating a smoother, quieter space, and then narrower again at the shoulders themselves, where a lot of movement is happening.

I have seen quite a number of variations of this poncho made by friends and knitting retreat participants. It looks very good, also, in dark and light gray colors. For a lighter, less warm version, single yarns could be used throughout the piece, and of course the length can be varied as well.

This poncho was knitted by our friend Denise.

DIAGRAM 10

Instructions:

Make a swatch with the yarns, knitting needles, and stitches indicated. If necessary, adjust the needle sizes to obtain proper gauge (see "Making Swatches," page 45, and "Adjusting Sizes," page 47).

Using the smaller circular needle, cast on 60 stitches using a single strand of the lighter color yarn. Join for working in the round, being careful not to twist the first row of stitches on the needle.

Purl 6 rounds.

Change to darker color yarn (single strand) and knit 1 round, then purl 2 rounds with lighter color yarn.

Now, slowly increase the number of the darker color knit rounds between the lighter color purl rounds. In this section, knit rounds are always executed with the darker color, purl rounds with the lighter color.

Knit 2 rounds, purl 2 rounds.
Knit 3 rounds, purl 2 rounds.
Knit 4 rounds, purl 2 rounds.

With the 5th knit section, the increases for the yoke begin.

Knit 4 rounds.

First increase round: Knit 15 stitches, M1. Repeat to the end of the round (64 stitches).

Purl 2 rounds.

Following this first increase round at the transitional space between the neck and the shoulders, you may use the formula of increasing 16 stitches in every 4th round. This formula is very flexible. For example, many more stitches could be increased in one round, and then no increases made for a while in the following rounds.

Where the instructions state to "add stitches," scatter these increases more or less evenly across the round. Use the M1 increase.

Continue to knit with the darker color and purl with the lighter color.

Knit 7 rounds, then add 16 stitches across the next round (80 stitches total).

Purl 2 rounds.

Knit 7 rounds, then add 32 stitches across the next round (112 stitches).

Purl 2 rounds.

Knit 3 rounds, add 32 stitches across the next round (144 stitches).

Switch to using a double strand of yarn in the darker color only, and to needle size 10 1/2, 29 inches long.

(The use of double yarns and bigger needles will add to the width of the yoke in this section.)

Purl 2 rounds.

You will be creating narrow bands of knit and purl stitches with the following repeated pattern: knit 2 rounds, purl 2 rounds.

Add 2 more increase rounds near the beginning of this section:

In the first round of the first knit band, add 32 stitches across the round (176 stitches).

In the first round of the third knit band, add 16 stitches across the round (192 stitches).

Continue working knit and purl bands to the desired length and bind off loosely.

To adjust the width according to your needs, make sure to try on the yoke and decide on the number of increase rounds you want to add.

Size and Design Adjustments:

Create your own poncho using the stitch pattern and color combination you prefer. Calculate the number of stitches to cast on for the cowl, according to your yarn and gauge. After completing the cowl, just follow the increase formula of adding 16 stitches every 4th round until the poncho is as wide as you would like, and then continue knitting to the desired length.

Extra-Warm Poncho Variation
Renate Hiller

Materials & Tools

Yarn: 12 oz, about 600 yds, bulky weight Elderlana from Viriditas Farm in California; 3 1/2 oz, about 125 yds, worsted-weight wool/mohair yarn

Needles: Circular knitting needles, size 11, 16 and 29 in. long; size 11 1/2, 29 in. long or longer

Gauge: 3 sts per inch with smaller needle, 2 1/2 sts per inch with larger needle

Color: At least two harmonizing colors in darker and lighter shades

I used: Cutch and black walnuts to overdye the gray tones of Elderlana, and separate cutch and black walnut baths to dye the wool/mohair yarn in two batches.

This poncho is modeled by our friend Laura. Viriditas Farm is known for growing colored cotton organically. The sheep on the farm eat down the plant stubble, reducing the need to use the tractor. Elderlana is yarn spun from the wool of the older sheep on the farm, who have spent their lives giving wool and doing soil preservation work. I was touched by their story on the farm's website.

This variation of the poncho is lighter and two inches shorter than the original design. I knitted the cowl and yoke with the size 11 needle and changed to size 11 1/2 at the transition from the yoke to the main body of the poncho. As in the original design, I played with purl ribs in knit textures and switched to an all-purl texture for the main body. I chose the purl texture to achieve a cocoon-like shape with a horizontal stitch alignment, and the typical curling under at the bottom edge. (A knit texture would show a vertical stitch alignment and would tend to curl outward.) The lustrous quality of the mohair yarn forms a nice contrast to the matte quality of the Elderlana yarn.

As in the original design, I cast on 60 stitches, but made increases only up to 144 stitches. This number gave sufficient width due to the bulky yarn and the larger needle size.

Seamless Sweater

Renate Hiller

Materials & Tools

Yarn: 116 oz, about 990 yds, worsted-weight wool/alpaca yarn

Needles: 4 circular knitting needles and 1 set of double-pointed needles: 3 circular, size 10, 16, 29, and 36 in. long; 1 circular size 8, 16 in. long, for the sleeves above the elbow; 1 set of 4 double-pointed needles in the same size as for the upper sleeves, for the sleeves below the elbow

Gauge: You will need to check your gauge two times: the stockinette portion of the body is at 4 sts per inch, and the sleeves are at 4 1/2 sts per inch

Color: Harmonizing shades of a single color and its neighbors on the color wheel

I used: A muted, rosy red color in various shades (dyed with brazilwood and black walnut) with purplish and golden/tan-colored accent rounds close to the face.

This comfortable sweater is knit in one piece, from the top down. The worsted-weight wool/alpaca yarn has a soft feel. The judicious use of garter stitch bands and single purl rounds within the overall stockinette texture makes for a harmonious design and allows for ease of movement.

The thought of knitting a sweater can be somewhat daunting. It is a large piece of knitting that needs to fit well and look good. Experienced knitters often tell stories about unfinished sweaters that were abandoned out of frustration. I remember my mother taking pity on me when I was growing up, finishing a sweater I could not face any longer.

However, knitting a sweater from the top down is a relatively easy task, especially after one has gone through the process of making a poncho in this way. This type of sweater can be started with a rolled edge or a band of ribbing, but it can also be started with a cowl.

I personally like the warmth of a cowl, and decided to begin my sweater with a cowl that would hug my neck closely but that could also be partially turned over to reveal the beginning of the pattern design. In this case, you are first knitting the part that will be showing and then the part that will be on the inside. I developed the design loosely described in the instructions for this first part, then used stockinette texture for the part that will be close to the neck. After the cowl was knitted to the correct length, I added an increase round of stitches to better accommodate the size of my head at the bind-off edge, then bound off the cowl with loose stitches. I then began the yoke part of the sweater by knitting onto the purl side of the cowl the same number of stitches that I had bound off, and continued by knitting the yoke in garter stitch (knit one round, purl one round) and garter stitch bands. These bands end with a single purl round below the chest and begin again in this way toward the bottom edge of the sweater.

Another possibility would be to begin the sweater with a provisional cast-on at the neck, and add the cowl after the main body of the sweater is finished.

The seemingly challenging problem of increases in the yoke can be solved by a simple formula: increase 4 stitches in every round between the neck and the shoulders. This formula I have learned by making increases for a raglan poncho, where I increased 4 times 2 stitches in every 2nd round. The application of this formula is very flexible and can be adapted to fewer increase rounds with more increases in each round, such as 16 stitches every 4th round, as I have done in this sweater. The important thing is to try on the piece as it grows to make sure that it will fit well.

Before determining the armhole division, I recommend that you try on the piece to see whether you need to add another increase round or not. The yoke needs to go over the shoulders so that there will be enough room for the movements of the arms later on. It is good to have a friend or family member help you at this important moment.

There are also different ways to end the sweater and the edges of the sleeves. These edges need to relate to the overall design and at the same time give stability to these areas that are the most vulnerable. Again, rolled edges, ribbing, and garter stitch bands can be used, and knit hemlines are also possible. I used widening garter stitch bands to relate to the overall design and prevent curling at the bottom edge.

Instructions:

Make a swatch with the yarns, knitting needles, and stitches indicated. If necessary, adjust the needle sizes to obtain proper gauge (see "Making Swatches," page 45, and "Adjusting Sizes," page 47).

Color changes are not detailed in these instructions. In general, bands of darker colored yarn were incorporated mostly at the edge of the cowl and at the bottom edges of the body and sleeves. For your own sweater, you can use a single-color yarn and play purely with texture, or incorporate different colors into your design.

Suggestions for textural changes are given, rather than strict instructions, with room left for your own individual choices.

The Cowl

Use the size 10, 16-inch circular needle and cast on 72 stitches using the knit-on method for its flexibility. Join for working in the round, being careful not to twist the first row of stitches on the needle. Work in garter stitch (knit 1 round, purl 1 round) for 4 rounds. Continue working the cowl, mostly with knit rounds, incorporating some purl rounds near the top if desired, until the piece measures 7 1/2 inches from cast-on edge. The lower part of the cowl should be all knit rounds (stockinette texture). Make the first increase round at the bottom of the cowl: *Knit 9 stitches, M1. Repeat from * 8 times (80 stitches). Bind off the cowl loosely.

The Yoke
To begin the yoke, knit into the purl side of the cowl, 80 stitches.
The top of the yoke is worked in garter stitch (knit 1 round, purl 1 round). All increases are made on knit rounds.
After 4 garter stitch rounds, begin yoke increases, using the rule of increasing 16 stitches in every 4th round. These increases can be scattered more or less evenly across the round.
As you increase, change to a longer circular needle when it becomes necessary.
After working the top of the yoke in garter stitch, you can change to mostly knit rounds with garter stitch inserts and single purl rounds as you wish.
After 10 increase rounds, you should have 240 stitches on the needle. Continue knitting until you come to the point where the sleeves should begin. Ideally, you should try on the sweater to determine this. Put some stitches on a string or on another circular needle to fit the yoke over your shoulders.

The Lower Body
On the next round, you will be starting at the center back of the sweater and separating off stitches to be knitted later for the sleeves.
With a circular needle, knit 35 stitches. Place 50 stitches on a string to hold them for the sleeve. Cast on 6 stitches using the knit-on method, then knit the next 70 stitches (pulling yarn to close the gap). Place the next 50 stitches on another string. Cast on 6 stitches using the knit-on method, then knit 35 stitches.
You will have 152 stitches on the circular needle (change to a shorter length as needed). Continue knitting, incorporating color and texture changes as desired, until the piece has the desired length. (Try on or compare with another sweater for fit.) On the last several rounds of the body, work garter stitch (knit one round, purl one round) for a non-curling edging that matches the cowl and the rest of the sweater. Bind off all stitches.

The Sleeves
Return to one set of sleeve stitches. Transfer stitches from the string to a size 8, 16-inch circular needle and knit these stitches. When you come to them, pick up and knit the 6 stitches across the cast-on edge at the base of the armhole, making sure to close the gap in the two corners, where the sleeve and the body connect.
You can do this by adding an extra stitch or two on either side.
Continue knitting every round to the elbow, incorporating color and texture changes to match the body if desired. Keep track of how many rounds you knit, for working the second sleeve.
On the next round, change to double-pointed needles. Place a marker at the middle of the underarm as a guide for the following decreases. At the beginning of the round, starting at the stitch marker, *k1 k2tog and at the end of the round, knit to 3 stitches before the marker, followed by ssk k1. (See "Decreases" on page 149 in the appendix.) Knit 3 rounds. Repeat from *, decreasing 2 stitches every 4 rounds, until the sleeve is the desired length and the wrist is the desired circumference; you may need to stop decreasing earlier, to avoid making the area around the wrist too tight, or work a few extra decreases toward the end for a tighter wrist section.
At the end of the sleeve, work several rounds of garter stitch (knit 1 round, purl 1 round) to match the body edging, then bind off.
Work the second sleeve to match the first.

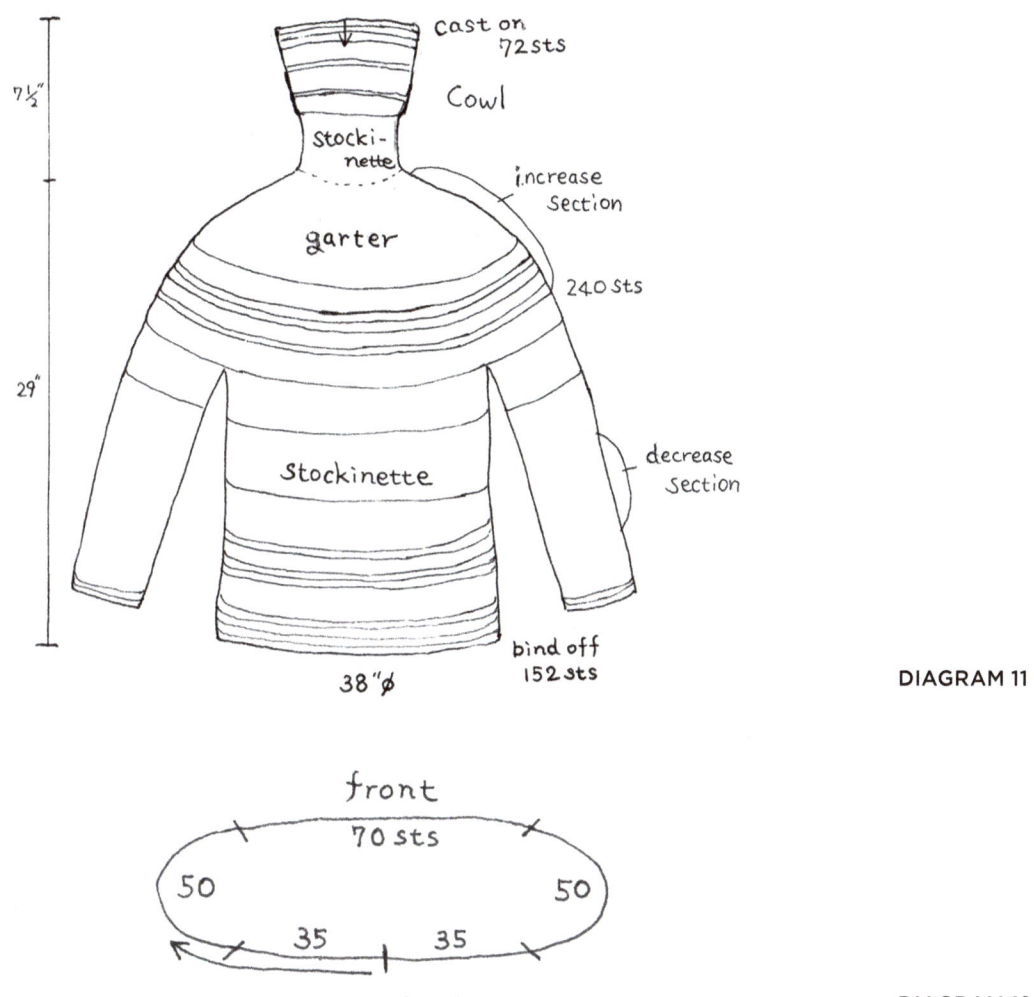

DIAGRAM 11

DIAGRAM 12

Size Adjustment

Knit with a different yarn and gauge and determine how many stitches you need to begin the cowl. The circumference of the cowl should be about 20 inches at the top edge.
Adjust the increase section if you need a narrower or wider yoke. Work more increases, or more increase rows, for a wider, deeper yoke, fewer for a smaller and shallower yoke.
The numbers for the armhole division can be adjusted. Use the diagram as a pattern for determining your own numbers. In general, about 1/6 of the total number of yoke stitches should be separated for each armhole, while the rest are divided between front and back.
For the sleeves, using a needle 2 sizes smaller than that used for the body makes the sleeves tighter to begin with. You can also knit with the same size needles as the body, and start decreasing earlier if needed.
As mentioned in the main instructions, you can adjust the decreases below the elbow to achieve the desired sleeve length and wrist circumference.
Always be sure to keep track of how you worked the first sleeve, so you can repeat it exactly with the second!

Seamless Sweater Variation 1

Renate Hiller

This variation has a simple, rolled-edge neckline, created by beginning with several knit rounds, and the sleeve and bottom hem have rolled edges as well. The texture is somewhat denser, as it is knit with size 8 needles and a gauge of 4 1/2 stitches per inch. This sweater is somewhat longer and roomier below the chest, and the sleeves were not decreased below the elbows, leaving them wider and looser at the wrists.

The overall stockinette texture is enhanced in the shoulder area by a rhythmic and dynamic sequence of double purl rounds with strongly colored accents. The colors are warm brownish/greenish/reddish tones that were dyed with cutch, madder, black walnut, and indigo. The strongly colored accent rounds are reddish/brownish tones, dyed with cutch only. The darker tones slowly increase towards the bottom of the sweater, creating interest in what is otherwise a simple stockinette texture.

Weaving in ends; Seamless Sweater Variation 3

Seamless Sweater Variation 2
Renate Hiller

This variation is modeled by our friend Sono.

For this version—with its beautiful cowl—I followed the general design of the original. What I played with here is the dynamic use of three colors, moving from the warmest color predominating in the cowl and chest area to cooler colors toward the bottom of the sweater and sleeves, with the warmest color reappearing at the edge of the sleeves. The bands of the coolest color begin in the cowl with purl rounds, ending with a round of k1, sl1 (knit one stitch, slip one stitch—slip purl-wise, with the yarn in the back); it is the opposite in the rest of the sweater, where the bands begin with a round of k1, sl1, and end with a single purl round in the otherwise all-knit texture. The k1, sl1 rounds make for gentle color transitions as the two colors used are alternating from stitch to stitch, and visually the single purl rounds create a kind of barrier at the edge of the color bands.

To finish the bottom edge of the sweater and the edges of the sleeves I used a knitted hem with a purl row as the edge, followed by a stockinette band. The knit stitches are not bound off but sewn onto the knitting with shallow stitching.

The dyes used to achieve the three colors were a combination of brazilwood and madder for the basic red and coreopsis flowers for the other two tones. Two thirds of the red yarn was overdyed in a bath of coreopsis flowers, and one half of that yarn was overdyed a second time in the same coreopsis bath.

Seamless Sweater Variation 3

Materials & Tools

Yarn: 14 1/2 oz of Clare's Corrie three-ply DK (double knit), 72 percent Corriedale and 28 percent Wensleydale mix, from Foster Sheep Farm, Schuylerville, New York; 1 1/2 oz of fine mohair bouclé in red and green from the Fiber Craft Studio

Needles: Circular knitting needles, size 8, 16 in. long and 29 in. long or longer; you will need to have 2 16-in needles for the arms, which are worked at the same time; 4 double pointed needles, size 8, for the sleeves below the elbows

Gauge: 5 sts per inch

Color: A variety of matching colors

We used: Wool yarns in greens and blues, with a sprinkling of reds and purples dyed at the farm with flowers and madder, and mostly overdyed with indigo, at the Fiber Craft Studio.

Our friend Laura is the model and creator of this sweater.

As always, as a warm-up practice and to obtain the correct gauge, make a swatch with the yarns, knitting needles, and type of stitches indicated. If necessary, adjust the needle size to obtain proper gauge (see "Making Swatches," page 45, and "Adjusting Sizes," page 47).

Laura began the sweater with a rolled edge and used single purl rounds in the overall stockinette texture. The striking feature of this sweater is the amazing color work. Laura played with five different green tones, a beautiful blue, a purple, and a red. The strong red makes an appearance close to the neck and is carried by the fine mohair bouclé. Another mohair bouclé in light green appears, here and there, over the entire sweater and the arms and—like the red bouclé—is carried together with the regular yarn.

Laura cast on 80 stitches on the 16-inch circular needle and knitted 3 inches for the rolled edge. She then increased 16 stitches, evenly spaced across the round, and came to a total of 96 stitches. She then knitted 4 rounds and started increasing 16 stitches every 4th round, up to a total of 11 increases and 262 stitches, switching to larger needles, of course, as required.

After trying on her piece, she determined to use 51 stitches for each sleeve, leaving 160 stitches for the body, and followed the instructions for the original design of the Seamless Sweater, above. She started the division at the center back and added 6 stitches each for the underarms. (See diagram 12, page 81, for a reference on where to place the division.)

After placing the stitches for the arms on 16-inch needles, she knit the body of the sweater at the same time as the two arms, alternating among a piece of the body and then a similar size piece of each arm. This allowed her to coordinate the color work between the body and the sleeves really well.

To start each sleeve, she moved the stitches from the scrap yarn to a 16-inch circular needle and added 2 stitches each on each side of the armhole to fill the gaps. After she reached the elbow of each sleeve, she started decreasing (see the decreases in the Seamless Sweater, above) every 8th round, 5 times in total.

Due to the stockinette texture, the sleeves have a rolled edge.

She finished the body of the sweater with a hem. (See Seamless Sweater Variation 2, on the previous page.)

PART TWO: THE KNITTING JOURNEY

Horizontal and Vertical Gestures: Knitting Back and Forth

The horizon is the line where heaven and earth seem to meet. Anything horizontal follows this line, and anything vertical is arranged perpendicular to this line.

Trees grow vertically toward the sky, and many of their branches and most of their leaves reach for the light in horizontal ways.

Human beings embody both vertical and horizontal dimensions: In our uprightness, we embody the vertical dimension, and with both arms stretched sideways we align with the horizontal, thus forming a cross.

In knitting garments, horizontal and vertical gestures arise when we create flat pieces by knitting back and forth, using two needles or a circular needle. These flat pieces can take on the form of scarves, shawls, or ponchos that can be worn loosely, following the contours of the body, or can be made into three-dimensional pieces by adding side seams to create holes for the arms, as in the case of tunics, vests, and boleros.

When we knit garments horizontally, starting from the bottom of one half of the garment and working upward, we may imagine the contours of the solid, dark ground beneath our feet. As the knitting progresses toward the upper body and the head, we may experience feelings of levity and of light. As we continue knitting the piece across the shoulders and down the back, we make the opposite journey from above to below. The front and back of the garment are knitted in sequence, one after the other. We may first knit the front and then the back, or we may proceed in the opposite way.

The different qualities we may imaginatively experience along this journey of making can be expressed artistically through color gradations and different textures related to weight or density. There is also the possibility of giving the back of the garment a darker, denser quality than the front.

When we knit vertically from side to side, symmetry between left and right comes strongly into play; the left needs to become a mirror image of the right, and vice versa.

We can bring in changes in color and texture that express the different qualities of the front and the back of the body, as well as the two sides. From the sleeves across the shoulders and moving toward the head, the color progressions can change from light to dark and back to light again. Colors and textures can also express movement and strength around the shoulders, and in general can relate to the shapes, movements, and forces of the body.

Introductory Project: Scarves

Scarves are simple, rectangular pieces that will allow you to explore the ways of working practiced throughout this section. If you take into account how they are worn, they offer many possibilities for working creatively with colors and stitches.

With the help of several knitted examples, we will guide you to explore the use of different stitch patterns and their practical and visual impact on your knitting, along with color gestures, color combinations, and transitions between colors.

We recommend that you create a few scarves before you make any of the other projects featured in this section.

Scarves are useful accessories that can be worn in all kinds of ways, and if made with appropriate materials, in all kinds of weather. Wrapped around the neck with both ends hanging down freely or tied into a knot, a long scarf can prevent cold air from migrating to the chest, shoulders, and back. Shorter scarves can bring warmth too, especially if they are wide enough to cover the back and shoulders.

Beyond their practical and useful applications, scarves have decorative functions as well. They can add beauty, harmony, and a hint of playfulness to any outfit. The soft draping of the fabric and colors close to the face can add a cheerful or festive note, soften or increase the formality of an outfit, or relate to the mood of the moment, the day, or the season. They bring a personal note to the pieces of clothing we wear.

Knitting Widthwise

A scarf worked widthwise in garter stitch is a wonderful project for a beginner. The scarf can be short or long, narrow or wide. All it takes is casting on a number of stitches, knitting back and forth until the desired length is reached, and finishing by binding off and securing the yarn ends with a darning needle.

To add more interest, we can introduce different stitches and colors into the design.

Scarf Design 1: Garter Stitch Scarf
Mikae Toma

Materials & Tools

Yarn: 5 oz, about 225 yds, worsted- to bulky-weight merino wool yarn

Needles: Straight knitting needles, size 8 (or size needed to obtain gauge)

Gauge: 4 1/2 sts per inch

Color: One darker color for the ends of the scarf, and a contrasting color in medium and lighter shades for the middle of the scarf

I used: Warm brown, dyed with black walnut, for the two ends, and two different tones of warm yellow, dyed with onion skins.

This scarf is knitted in garter stitch all the way through. As it is knitted row by row to build the length, color changes can be made across the knitting in any row. It can be worn simply, with two ends hanging down, or the two ends can be tied below the chin. It can also be wrapped twice around the neck.

After casting on, I began knitting with the darker colored yarn, which emphasizes that this part is at the bottom. After about 6 1/2 inches of knitting, I started using lighter colors. For the middle of this piece, thinking about how this part touches the neck and drapes around the face, I changed to the lightest color. When changing colors, I knitted two rows with the new color followed by two rows of the old color, and then continued using the new color. In this way I achieved gradual color transitions. These transitions look different depending which side of the scarf one starts them on. I always started the color changes on the same side of the scarf, so that each side would have a consistent appearance.

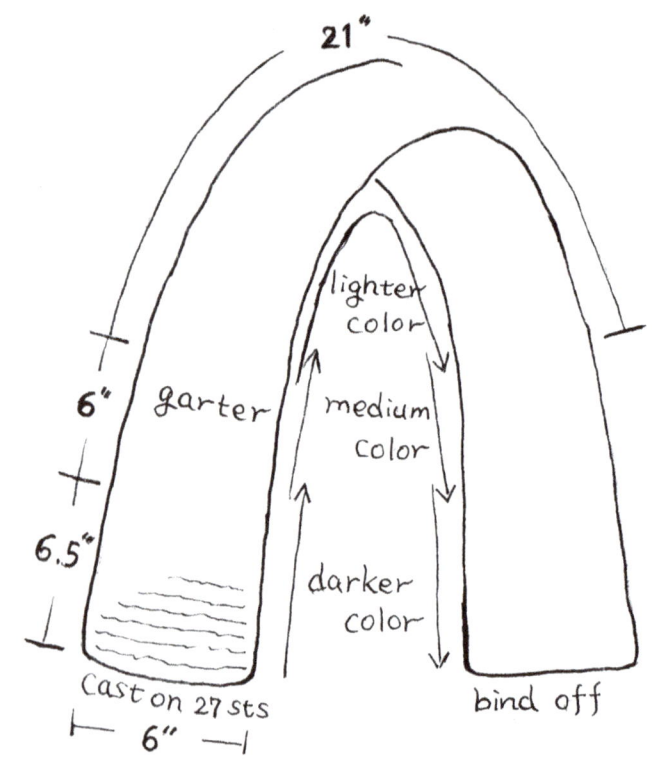

DIAGRAM 13

Instructions:

Cast on 27 stitches, using the darker color.
Knit every row until the piece measures about 6 1/2 inches, after knitting an even number of rows.
Switch to the medium shade of the other yarn and knit 2 rows.
Switch to darker color yarn and knit 2 rows.
Switch back to medium color and continue knitting every row for about 6 more inches, for an even number of rows.
Knit 2 rows in the lightest color, then 2 rows in the medium color, then continue knitting with the lightest color for 21 inches.
Reverse the pattern for the other end of the scarf, always changing colors after an even number of rows.
When the last section is complete, bind off all stitches loosely. Weave in yarn ends.

Scarf Design 2: Ribbed Scarf

Mikae Toma

This scarf is knitted with alternating knit and purl stitches to create a ribbed texture. Ribbing pulls the stitches tightly together, which adds thickness to the scarf, but makes it narrower in width. The texture of ribbing emphasizes verticality and creates elasticity, which brings a wonderful flow when the scarf is wrapped around the neck. This narrow but long scarf can be wrapped twice around the neck.

Materials & Tools

Yarn: 4 1/2 oz, approximately 440 yds, sport-weight wool/mohair yarn

Needles: Straight knitting needles, size 6 (or size needed to obtain gauge)

Gauge: 8 1/2 sts per inch

Color: Three darker to lighter tones of the same color

I used: A warm reddish color, dyed with madder root.

The wool/mohair yarn is a little fluffy, which brings a soft and gentle look to the scarf.

Considering the fact that ribbing pulls the stitches together, I cast on a relatively high number of stitches. In order to make smooth edges, I slipped the first stitch of each row (that is, I put the right needle through the first stitch on the left needle as if to purl, but rather than making a new loop, simply transferred the stitch from the left to the right needle).

I lived strongly with the question of color changes, considering where to place darker and lighter colors so they would harmonize with the placement of the scarf on the body. I began with the darker color at one end to bring a sense of heaviness at the bottom and then changed to the medium color to form a kind of bridge to the lighter color at the center of the scarf, which when worn is close to the face. I intended to make a scarf long enough to wrap twice around the neck. As the piece grew, I tried it on many times to see the arrangement of those colors, making sure to bring lightness close to the face.

I always changed the color on the same side, just as I did with the Garter Stitch Scarf. In order to avoid a sudden change of color, I knitted two rows with the new color, two rows with the previous color, then continued knitting with the new color.

In ribbed texture, the color changes look the same on the front side as on the back side.

Instructions:

With the darkest color yarn, cast on 50 stitches.
* Slip the first st only, p1, k1, p1, repeat from * to end of row. Continue working all rows in this way, creating a ribbed texture.
After about 11 inches, switch to medium color yarn.
Work 2 rows in medium color, then switch back to the darkest color and work 2 rows.

Switch to medium color and continue working ribbed texture for about 10 inches.
Switch to lighter color, creating color change in the same way.
Work about 23 1/2 inches in lightest color, then reverse the color changes for the other end of the scarf.
When final section is complete, bind off all stitches and weave in yarn ends.

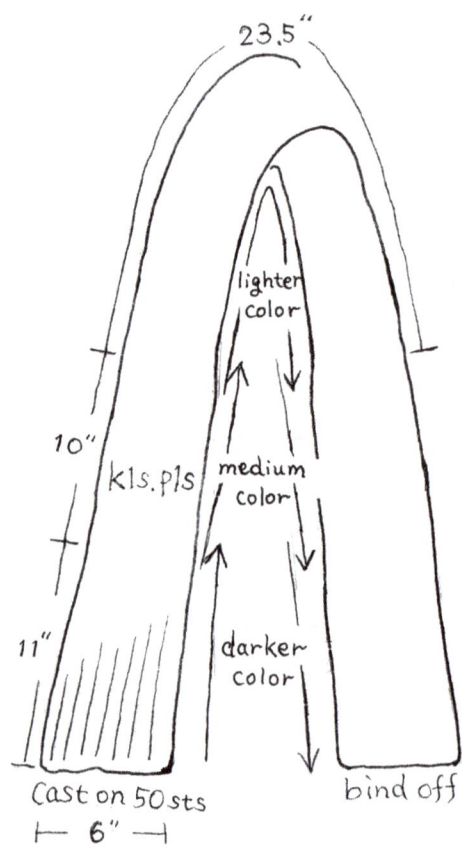

DIAGRAM 14

Scarf Design 3: Scarf with Garter Stitch and Ribbing

Mikae Toma

I created this scarf by exploring a combination of garter stitch and ribbed textures.
A garter stitch texture forms horizontal lines, whereas rows of ribbing form vertical lines. These different qualities allowed me to introduce interesting effects on the different parts of the scarf.

This scarf is worn with the ribbed section around the neck, while the two ends with garter stitch hang down freely or are overlapped to warm the chest.

For this piece, I chose a relatively large sized needle to make the fabric of the scarf more flexible.

To begin the scarf, I simply knitted a number of rows to create a garter stitch section with the darker color yarn. When I felt this section was long enough, I introduced one row of ribbing (k1, p1) across the width of the scarf, and then went back to garter stitch for a few rows before working another row of ribbing. As the piece grew, I reduced the size of the garter stitch sections and kept the one row of ribbing separating these sections the same.

Materials & Tools

Yarn: 3 1/2 oz, about 220 yds, worsted-weight wool yarn

Needles: Straight knitting needles, size 9 (or size needed to obtain gauge)

Gauge: 4 sts per inch

Color: One main color, with a darker accent color for the ends

I used: A warm, golden yellow dyed with onion skin for the main color, with some of the yarn overdyed with indigo to create a darker, greenish tone for the accent color.

It was exciting to see how even just a few rows of ribbing placed at small intervals within the garter stitch section brought a gradual reduction of the width.

As the width began decreasing, I switched to the lighter color yarn and then gradually increased the length of the ribbing sections. I separated these growing sections by introducing two knit rows between them, which created a garter stitch rib across the width. For the middle section of the scarf, which would be wrapped around the neck, I worked with pure ribbing and then repeated the design in reverse order to create the second half of the scarf.

This design brought about great flexibility, especially in the areas where the ribbing predominates.

As the design metamorphoses from the two ends to the center, it changes gradually from the garter stitch section, with its horizontal linear quality, to the ribbing, with its vertical lines, and from a feeling of heaviness to lightness, from an almost static quality to a sense of movement.

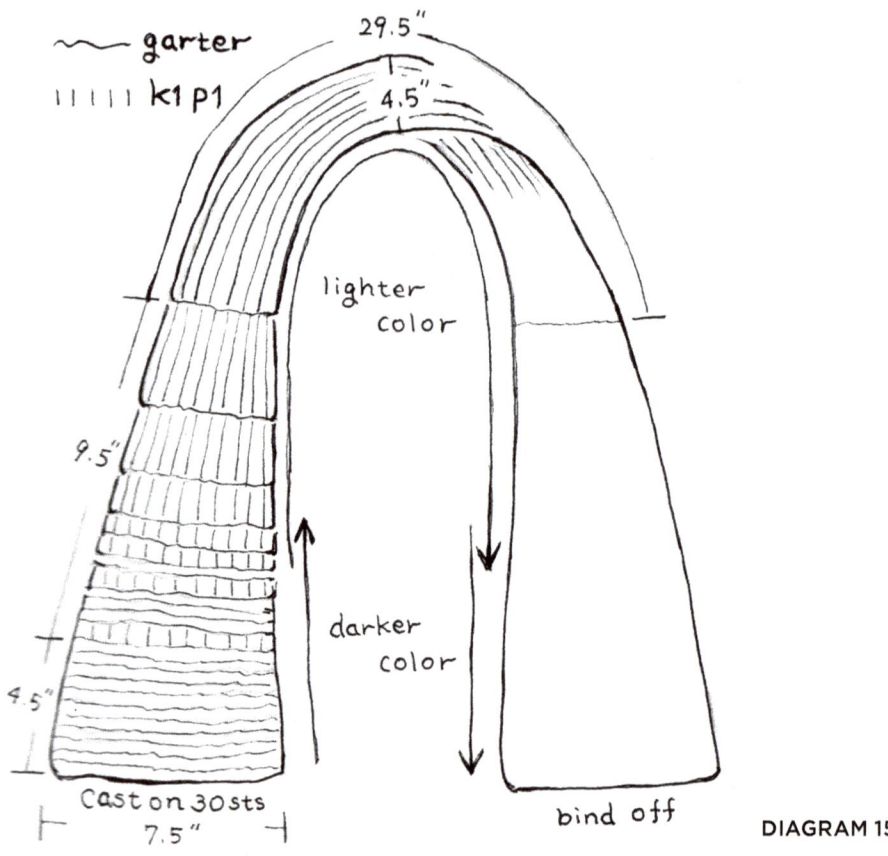

DIAGRAM 15

Instructions:

With the darker accent color, cast on 30 stitches.
Knit every row until the piece measures about 4 1/2 inches from the cast-on edge.
On the next row, k1, p1, repeat to end of row.
Knit 9 more rows.
On the next row, k1, p1, repeat to end of row.
Switch to the lighter, main color and knit 2 rows.
Switch to the darker color and knit 4 rows.
On the next row, switch to the lighter color, k1, p1, repeat to end of row.
Then, again, switch to the darker color to knit 2 rows.
Switch back to the lighter color, k1, p1, repeat to the end, and knit 1 row.
K1, p1, repeat to the end, and knit 3 rows.
Knit 1 row.
K1, p1, for 5 rows.
Knit 1 row.
K1, p1, for 7 rows.
Knit 1 row.
K1, p1, for 11 rows.
Knit 1 row.
K1, p1, for 29 1/2 inches.
Continue, reversing the instructions above to make the second end of the scarf a mirror image of the first: Knit 1 row, then 11 rows of k1, p1; knit 1 row, then 7 rows of k1, p1; and so on.

From Scarf to Jacket

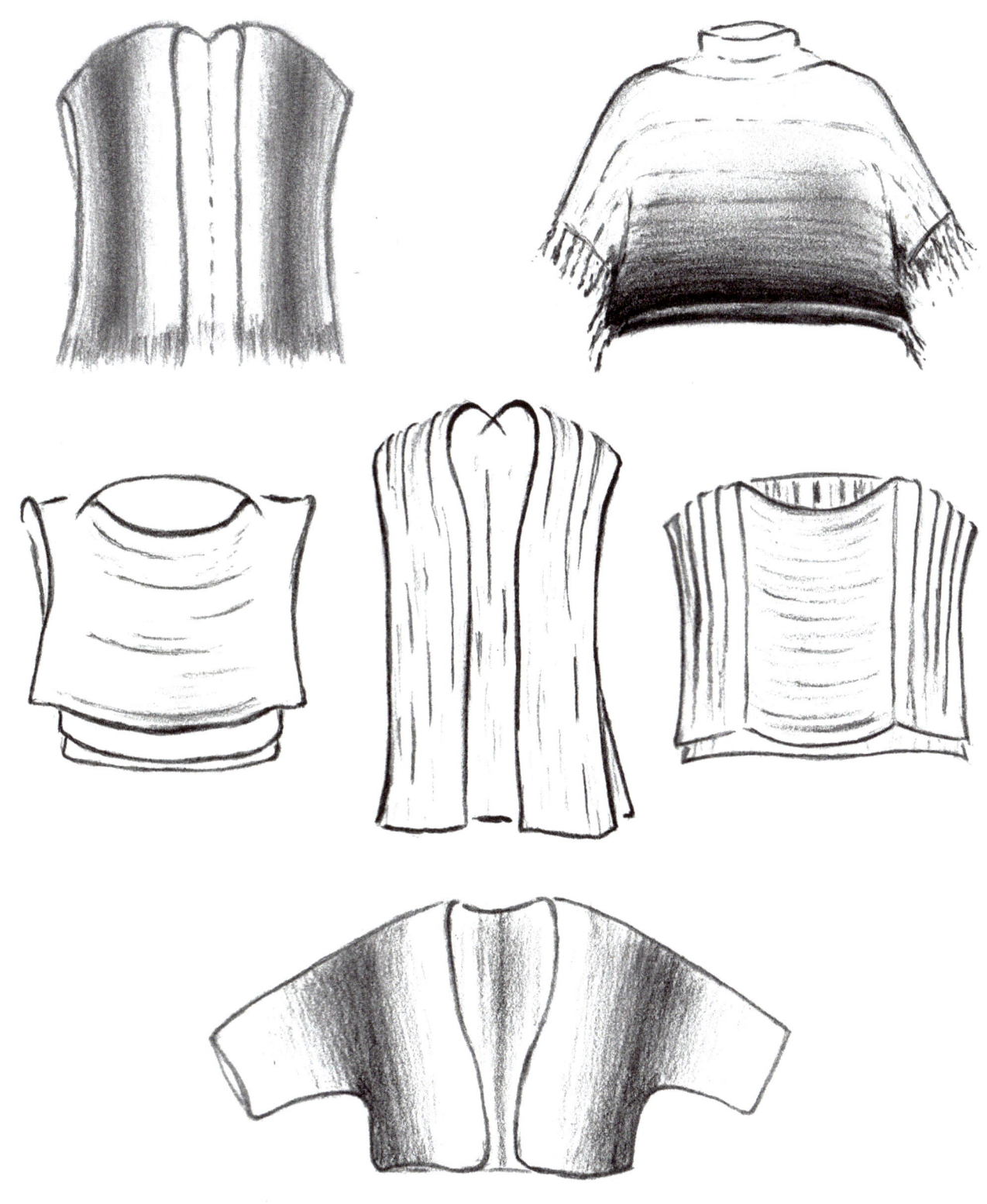

HORIZONTAL AND VERTICAL GESTURES: FROM SCARF TO JACKET

Long Scarf

Renate Hiller

This scarf is modeled by our friend Sono. It can be an accessory for a sweater or a coat. It is long enough to be wrapped around the neck for extra warmth. The subtle luster of the mohair and the curlicues in the bouclé yarn give the piece an almost festive flair.

Knitting a scarf lengthwise with garter stitch is as easy as knitting widthwise, but calls for handling many stitches. Knitting back and forth on a circular needle, without joining the stitches for knitting in the round, makes this possible.

It was an exciting moment when we encountered the idea of knitting scarves lengthwise and creating fringes in the process. A whole world of ideas opened up, as you can see in the following examples. The technique made possible wonderful gifts, as well as a number of hat and scarf combinations.

The magic of this process is manifold, as you will experience yourself once you get started. The lengthwise ridges of the garter stitch lend themselves to the subtle weaving together of various colors. In the fringes, the individual yarns that were laced together in the knitting become visible, giving a glimpse of the original materials that have been transformed through the process of creation. This is a place where knitting resembles weaving, as we often see the fringes of the weft in a finished woven piece.

The fringes are created by starting each row with a new piece of yarn, leaving a tail several inches long, and ending each row by cutting the yarn and leaving another tail of the same length. After ending a row, the last two fringes are knotted together with an overhand knot. This helps to hold everything well in place.

For these pieces, all kinds of fine- to worsted-weight yarns can be used, and bouclé yarns can add subtle textures and color variations. These are good projects for leftover yarns.

For the Long Scarf I chose worsted-weight yarns and a relatively large-sized needle to make the scarf soft and comfortable to wear. When considering how the colors would be arranged, I decided on a symmetrical design, mirrored on either side of the lengthwise center line of the scarf. This called for darker colors (strong purples and browns, with yellow highlights) on the outer edges to express firmness and a quality of strength, and lighter colors toward the center (subtle reds with a hint of lavender), expressing both softness and warmth.

The lavender-colored bouclé echoes the purples of the outer edges and adds to the quality of softness.

Playing with colors and textures has never been more satisfying!

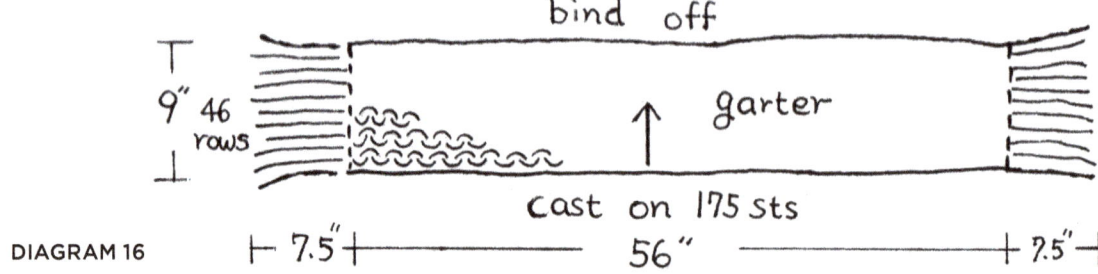

DIAGRAM 16

Materials & Tools

Yarn: 5 oz, about 300 yds, worsted-weight wool/mohair yarn in various colors; 1/2 oz mohair bouclé yarn

Needles: Circular knitting needle, size 10 1/2, 29 in. long

Gauge: 3 sts per inch

Color: A mix of solid or variegated yarns in harmonizing and/or complementary colors and darker and lighter shades

I used: Purples and browns at the edges, with yellow ribs on either side and light reds and lavenders towards the center, dyed with brazilwood, indigo, onion skins, and black walnut hulls.

Instructions:

Make a swatch with the yarns, knitting needles, and stitches indicated. If necessary, adjust the needle size to obtain proper gauge (see "Making Swatches," page 45, and "Adjusting Sizes," page 47).

With the color you have decided on for the outer edges of the scarf, cast on 175 stitches on a circular needle, leaving a tail of 7 1/2 inches, or the desired length for the fringes. Cut the yarn at the other end, leaving a tail of the same length.

Do not join for working in the round, but turn the needle to knit a flat piece, knitting back and forth.

On the next row, knit with a new strand of yarn, leaving tails at each end. Each set of two tails should be tied in an overhand knot to secure them.

Continue knitting every row, changing colors as desired.

When the piece measures about 4 1/2 inches, or is half as wide as the desired width of the scarf, reverse the order of colors, now moving from lighter to darker shades.

When the piece measures 9 inches from the cast-on edge or has the desired width, bind off all stitches loosely. Trim fringes if necessary.

Curved Shawl

Renate Hiller

Materials & Tools

Yarn: 5 oz, about 300 yds, worsted-weight wool/mohair yarn

Needles: Circular knitting needles, sizes 10 1/2 and 8, 29 in. long

Gauge: 3 sts per inch with larger sized needle

Color: A mix of solid or variegated yarns in harmonizing or complementary colors, and darker and lighter shades

I used: Browns and reds for an initial dark, strong edge, followed by pastel greens, reds, violets, and a sprinkling of pale yellow dyed with madder, Osage orange, indigo, and black walnut hulls.

This shawl, with its curved shape, drapes nicely over the shoulders. It brings warmth to the back, shoulders, and upper arms. It can be an extra layer in any season, although the colors I have chosen for this example give a fresh spring and early summer quality.

Although the technical process of knitting this shawl is the same as the process I used for the Long Scarf, namely, knitting back and forth in garter stitch leaving fringes of yarn at either end, it required quite a shift in consciousness. Rather than imagining and working toward a rectangular, symmetrical design, as I did before, I now pictured a curved, almost cape-like shape that would drape nicely over the shoulders. To achieve this shape, I imagined knitting in a horizontal direction from the bottom up, over the shoulder blades and upper arms toward the neck. I also used two needles of different sizes: a larger needle to begin with, which I used for about two thirds of the width of the scarf, and a smaller needle with which I knitted the remaining third.

This design also called for a different choice of colors with regard to dark and light. I started with dark, strong colors at the bottom and progressed toward lighter colors at the neck.

Additional gentle blocking (see "On Blocking and Caring for Your Woolen Knits" in the appendix on page 150) helped to emphasize the curved nature of the shawl.

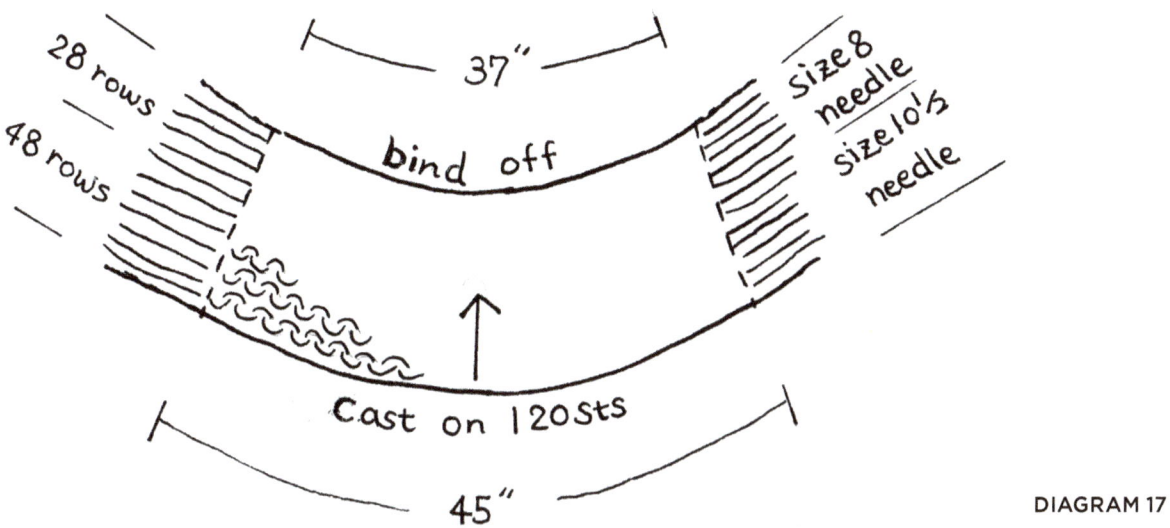

DIAGRAM 17

Instructions:
Make a swatch with the yarns, knitting needles, and stitches indicated. If necessary, adjust the needle sizes to obtain proper gauge (see "Making Swatches," page 45, and "Adjusting Sizes," page 47).

Cast on 120 stitches, using the darkest color yarn and larger sized circular needle. Work as for the Long Scarf, except that the colors are graded from dark to light across the width of the shawl, rather than mirrored across a central line.

After completing 48 rows, or about 2/3 of the desired width of the scarf, change to the smaller-sized needle.

Knit 28 more rows, bind off all stitches, and trim fringes.

Two-Shawls Vest

Renate Hiller

Materials & Tools

Yarn: 110 oz, about 600 yds, worsted-weight wool/mohair yarn in various colors

Needles: Circular knitting needles, sizes 10 1/2 and 9, 19 in. long

Gauge: 3 sts per inch with larger size needle

Color: One main color in a variety of shades, light to dark; an accent color in a second single, uniform shade

I used: Light to dark shades of green, with beige as a secondary color, dyed with Osage orange, indigo, and cutch.

This vest is modeled by our friend Janet. Two Curved Shawls (above, page 96) are joined to each other to make this vest. It is a wonderful layering piece that adds just enough warmth on cooler days in the summer, fall, or spring.

When the Curved Shawl was finished, I tried out different ways of wearing it and, as I placed it over one shoulder—voilà, I had one side of a vest. I placed the longer side close to the neck, and the shorter side over the upper arm; it draped really well. I was inspired to create two more Curved Shawls, but now with the idea of putting them together to make a vest.

In keeping with the function of a vest, I needed to take a different inner approach to knitting and the use of color than I had done with the Curved Shawl. First, I needed to picture the end result of my knitting. Rather than a shawl meant to drape horizontally over both shoulders, I would first create a piece that would be placed vertically over one shoulder and then a second piece for the other shoulder.

 To give the vest a protective and "settled" feeling, I chose beige and green tones, with the beige appearing rhythmically every second row. The green tones progress from light to dark and then to light again. I began each shawl with lighter greens on the edge that would be nearest to the neck and chest, moving into darker greens that would spread over the shoulders to express firmness and strength, and then lighter green tones again, to suggest openness around the arms. After binding both pieces off, I pinned them together with safety pins in the back and on the sides to establish the sewing lines. Then, using the mattress stitch, I sewed the two pieces together along the back seam; after that, I sewed the side seams as well. I lightly blocked (see "On Blocking and Caring for Your Woolen Knits" in the appendix on page 150) the finished piece on a dress form and cut the fringes to the length I liked.

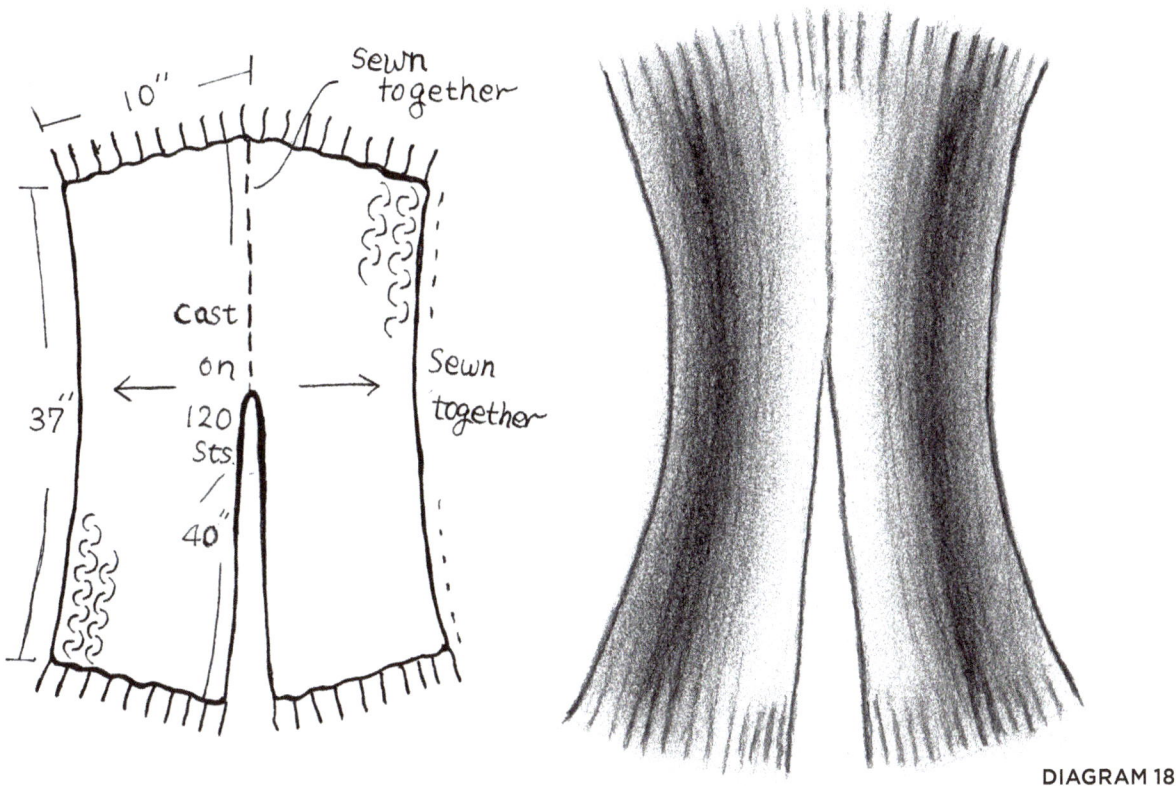

DIAGRAM 18

Instructions:

Make a swatch with the yarns, knitting needles, and stitches indicated. If necessary, adjust the needle sizes to obtain proper gauge (see "Making Swatches," page 45, and "Adjusting Sizes," page 47).

With the lightest shade of the main color yarn and the larger sized circular needle, cast on 120 stitches.

Knit as if making a Curved Shawl, but in placing the colors, work from light to dark and back to light again. Work in the accent color every second row.

When the shawl is complete, knit a second shawl in the same way.

Determine where the neck opening should begin, slightly less than halfway along the length of the scarves. Sew together along the back.

Determine the desired width of the arm openings, ideally by draping the vest over the body. Sew together each piece along the side seams.

Two-Shawls Vest Variation 1
Renate Hiller

I made this hand-spun version from the fleece of a Jacob sheep spun with the drop spindle.

It is quite sheer, has wider panels, and drapes beautifully across the shoulders. I sorted the locks according to color (beige, grays, and browns) and spun them into fine- to worsted-weight yarn. I dyed small skeins of the yarn with cutch and black walnut hulls. The short side seams were sewn together on the outside of the piece using a backstitch, about 2 inches from the side edges and 4 inches from the bottom.

Two-Shawls Vest Variation 2
Renate Hiller

This variation, modeled by our friend Janet, was knitted by our friend Laura.

Laura decided to cast on 128 stitches to make the piece somewhat longer. This added about 3 inches to the overall length of each panel. In addition to the regular wool/mohair yarns in rust and green colors, she introduced fine mohair and mohair bouclé yarns in brown, tan, and natural tones. She knitted these together with the wool/mohair yarns to embellish the left and right center parts of the vest, as well as the sides and arm openings.

These variations show how you can vary your own Two-Shawls Vest in many ways. You can make the pieces shorter or longer, wider or narrower, using different yarn weights and different gauges, creating a fabric that is denser or more sheer. Enjoy these explorations!

Short Poncho

Mikae Toma

Materials & Tools

Yarn: 16 oz single-ply spindle-spun yarn

Needles: Circular knitting needles: size 10, 36 in. long; size 10 1/2, 16 in. long for the neck

Gauge: 3 sts per inch

Color: Subtle shades of a single color

I used: Various shades of gray-brown from a Jacob sheep's fleece, dyed in chamomile, madder root, yellow cosmos, and black walnut; all of these yarns were then overdyed lightly with black walnut.

This short poncho, which is similar to a flat piece of woven cloth, is a simple but playful garment to make and wear.

It is knitted with single-ply yarns in garter stitch, starting from the bottom of the back, going up to the shoulders—which lays the foundation for the neck opening—and continuing down to the bottom front. As with the lengthwise-knitted scarves, the colors are changed after each row, leaving a couple of inches of yarn at the beginning and end of each row to create fringes.

Using wool fleece from a local farm and dyes derived from local plants makes me feel at one with the environment. I spun the yarn for this piece with a drop spindle, after careful preparation by washing, sorting, and carding with hand carders. When I am spinning with a drop spindle, I feel a close connection with the materials that I am transforming. It always amazes me to observe how the mass of fibers in my hand is slowly twisted into a spiraling strand of yarn by the rotating spindle. As I hold the spindle, suspended between heaven and earth, and observe the spiraling growth movement of the yarn, I feel a special connection with the creative forces in the universe.

While I was engaged in spinning, dyeing, and knitting this piece, I was able to tune into the creative forces alive in me at every step along the way. It was such a joy to leave a couple of inches of yarn at the beginning and end of each row, so that the textures of the hand-spun yarns remained visible. The yarn ends beautifully extended the width of the poncho.

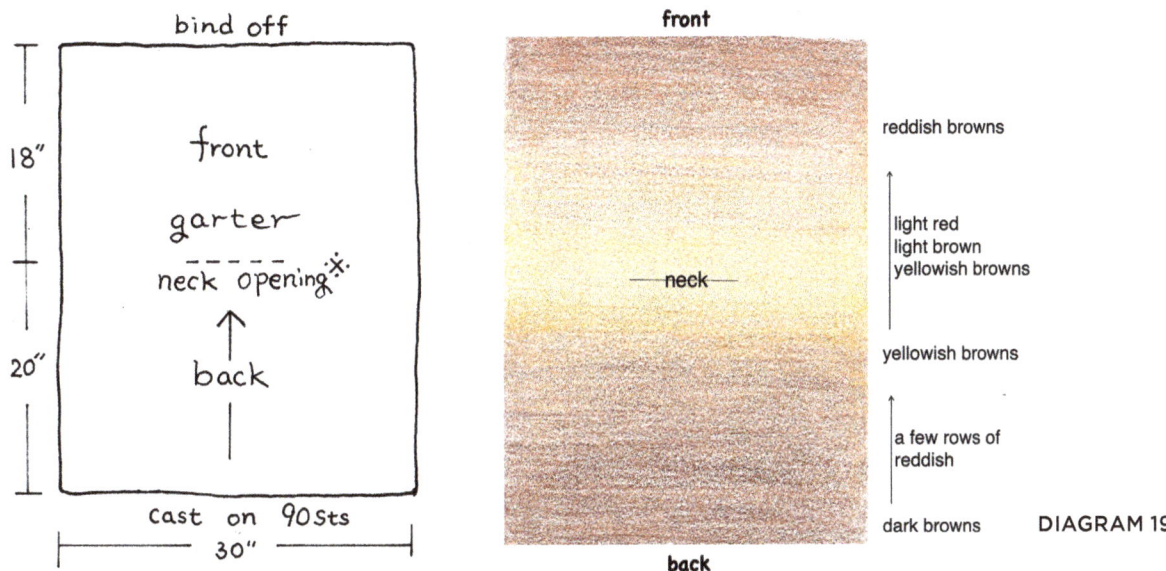

DIAGRAM 19

As I sorted a basket of small balls of yarn from darker to lighter colors, I grouped the colors for the back and the front of the piece into two batches to create a gradation of color. This creative process allowed me to develop a sense for the meaningful placement of the colors.

I thought that the back of the poncho should be a little longer and darker than the front. Here, a couple of different shades of brown were chosen to express a subtle gradation of dark to light. I wanted to bring more openness to the front side, as well as a feeling of movement, especially around the chest area. For this, I chose lighter and brighter shades.

The big question was how to place the colors around the shoulders, with their strength and potential for movement. The shoulder area is the transition from the back to the front, and it is the uppermost part of the garment when it is worn. So, I was torn between the ideas of expressing strength with the darker shades, or using lighter shades for a smooth transition toward the front. Making a color pencil drawing was very helpful for finding a balance.

Thicker yarn can be used toward the bottom edges to give weight, and thinner yarn can be used to bring a delicate and light effect around the face.

Instructions:
Make a swatch with the yarns, knitting needles, and stitches indicated. If necessary, adjust the needle sizes to obtain proper gauge (see "Making Swatches," page 45, and "Adjusting Sizes," page 47).
Before knitting the poncho, spend some time planning your color scheme. A color drawing like the one above can be helpful.
With the color you have designated for the bottom back of the poncho, cast on 90 stitches. Knit every row to create a garter stitch texture, changing yarn on each row and leaving a tail on each end (see instructions for Long Scarf, page 94).

Continue until the piece measures about 20 inches from the neck to the bottom, or has the desired length.

For the neck opening, knit 1/3 of the stitches using the main working yarn (30 stitches). Then take a separate piece of yarn in a different color to serve as a placeholder, and, leaving your main working yarn aside, use this placeholder yarn to knit 30 stitches in the center of the piece.

Cut this yarn, leaving a good length of tail on each side.

Pass the 30 stitches from the right needle to the left needle and reknit them using the main yarn. Continue knitting to end of row.

Continue knitting as before, following your planned color scheme for the front of the poncho.

When the piece measures 18 inches from the neck opening or has the desired length for the front, bind off all stitches.

Pull out the placeholder yarn from the neck opening and pick up the stitches from both front and back of the opening using a 16-inch circular needle.

Work a few rows of garter stitch in the round—knit one round, purl one round—to make a short and loose turtleneck.

Variation 1: Hand-spun Romney Poncho
Mikae Toma

This poncho is made in the same way as the Short Poncho (above, page 102), but it is wider and longer and has no fringes.

To make a poncho without fringes, simply weave in yarn ends left from color changes on the inner side of the poncho.

The single-ply yarns were spun in sport weight, using a drop spindle. The natural brown wool from Romney fleeces was sorted from light to dark shades.

Variation 2: Linen Vest

Mikae Toma

This vest is modeled by our friend Miho. This linen vest is a perfect piece for the spring and summer seasons.

The fine linen threads bring a kind of crispness to the texture of the knitting, and they soften over time, with wearing.

I created the linen vest in much the same way as the ponchos, but I sewed the sides together. The three-ply yarn for this variation was dyed with onion skins and an iron mordant. I started the knitting at the bottom of the front, and I introduced rows of purl stitches in an overall stockinette fabric at various intervals, bringing a rhythmic, dynamic feeling to the front.

I applied a progression from garter stitch to reverse stockinette to the back, with the armhole opening corresponding to the transition.

For the neck opening, after pulling out the placeholder yarn, I bound off the stitches for the front neckline loosely, and the stitches of the back a bit more tightly. The sides were then sewn together up to the armholes.

These variations show some possibilities for varying the Short Poncho design. As with the Two-Shawl Vest, you can use different yarns and different gauges, and can make the piece wider or narrower, longer or shorter.

Long Vest

Mikae Toma

Materials & Tools

Yarn: 8 oz, about 650 yds, lightweight linen and cotton blend yarn (of a hand-spun quality)

Needles: Circular knitting needle, size 10 1/2, 29 in. long; a second needle for holding stitches (can be smaller size)

Gauge: 3 sts per inch

Color: A neutral or other single shade of color

I used: Yarn dyed with black walnut in brownish tones.

This piece is loosely knitted in stockinette stitch, which creates a vertical grain with soft rolled-in edges for the armholes and in the two front panels. I began at the bottom edge of the back.

What makes this vest unique are the overlapping sections at the back of the neck, which allow the two front sections to separate and drape over the shoulders and around the neck in beautiful ways.

For quite a while I thought about making a long, lightweight vest, a layering piece that could visually unite the top and bottom garments of an outfit in a harmonious way. To highlight the hand-spun quality and texture of the yarn, I decided to knit loosely with a relatively large-sized knitting needle. The stockinette texture, especially when knitted loosely, emphasizes the vertical lines of the stitches, which was just what I wanted for this piece. As I was knitting the back panel, I was pleased with the effect of the rolled-in side edges—the result of the stockinette texture, which brought a beautiful softness. I thought this effect would be lovely for the edges of the two front panels as well; however, it would also make them quite a bit narrower.

As I was knitting up the back, I wondered how to achieve the separation into two side-panels. What could I do around the neckline? Looking at the back of a dress form, I focused on the transition from the back to the two separate shoulders, with the neck arising in the middle, and thought about the movements of the arms. Suddenly, the simple gesture of one panel crossing over another came to my mind.

To achieve such a crossover, I picked up stitches on the reverse side of the piece and added them to the knitting needle. The two front panels partially overlap at the point behind the neck where they arise, forming a beautiful triangle that also makes this special place strong and durable. The overlap also added more stitches to the front panels and made them wider. When this piece is worn, it falls beautifully due to the loose quality of the fabric, and the overlapping triangle resonates with the structure of this special place on the body.

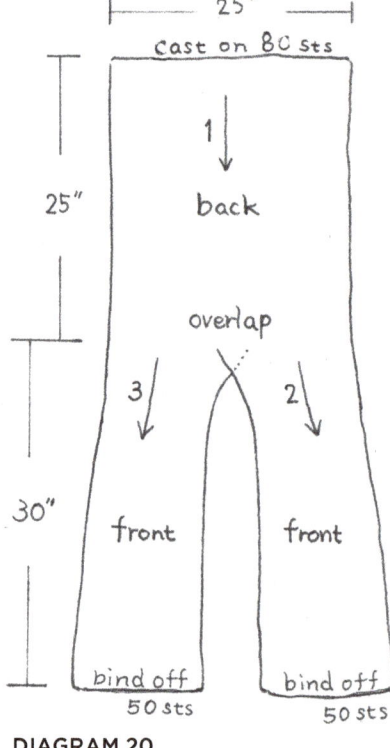

DIAGRAM 20

Instructions:

Make a swatch with the yarns, knitting needles, and stitches indicated. If necessary, adjust the needle size to obtain proper gauge (see "Making Swatches," page 45, and "Adjusting Sizes," page 47).

For the back, cast on 80 stitches. Work stockinette stitch (knit on right side, purl on wrong side) until the piece measures 25 inches from the cast-on edge. On the next purl row, purl 50 stitches. Leave the remaining 30 stitches on a second needle (can be a smaller size).

Work 50 stitches of the left front panel in stockinette stitch until the piece measures 30 inches from the start of the overlap.

Bind off all stitches.

Return to the stitches left on the second needle. Starting on the reverse (purl) side of the work, pick up 20 stitches in the fabric, beginning from the end of the stitches on the needle (see "Overlapping" on page 150 in the appendix). Turn the work and knit all stitches on the needle to begin the front panel. 50 stitches.

Continue working back and forth on these 50 stitches in stockinette stitch until the length matches the left front panel.

Bind off all stitches.

On a dress form or over the body, drape the vest and determine where armholes should fall. Mark this point with a safety pin. Sew side seams from this point to desired length. Several inches may be left open at the bottom.

Size Adjustment

According to your yarn and gauge, calculate the number of stitches you need to cast on for the back of the vest. Knit to the desired length up to the back of the neck. From here, decide how many stitches will belong to the overlap—around 5 to 6 inches worth, according to the sample garment; however, you may need more for a very wide neck or fewer for a narrow one. Set aside this number of stitches as you create the neck opening, as described above. Finish knitting the front of the vest, again to the desired length.

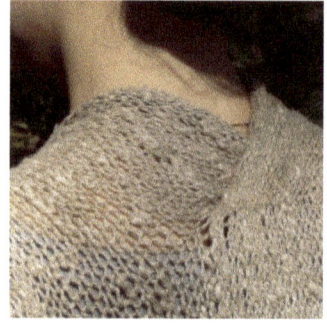

Overlap Tunic

by Mikae Toma

Materials & Tools

Yarn: 8 oz, about 600 yds, lightweight linen and cotton blend yarn of a hand-spun quality

Needles: Circular knitting needle, size 11, 29 in. long; a second needle for holding stitches (can be a smaller size)

Gauge: 3 sts per inch

Color: A neutral or other single color

I used: Yarn dyed with fermented persimmon in Japan.

This tunic—with two overlaps—developed from the Long Vest (above, page 107).

As visible in the drawing, the back overlap is shallower than the front overlap, and for good balance, the two overlaps change direction. This tunic is worked from the front to the back, rather than from back to front.

Instructions:

Make a swatch with the yarns, knitting needles, and stitches indicated. If necessary, adjust the needle sizes to obtain proper gauge (see "Making Swatches," page 45, and "Adjusting Sizes," page 47).

For the front, cast on 69 stitches. Work stockinette stitch (knit one row, purl one row) until the piece measures 20 inches from the cast-on edge.

On the next purl row, purl 48 stitches. Place the remaining 21 stitches on a second needle (can be a smaller size).

Continue to work stockinette stitch over the first 48 stitches for the right shoulder panel until the piece measures 13 inches from the start of the panel.

Break yarn and transfer these stitches to a length of yarn for holding.

Return to the 21 stitches placed on the second needle. Starting on the reverse side of the piece, pick up 27 stitches from the edge of the stitches on the needle (see "Overlapping" on page 150 in the appendix).

Turn the work and knit all stitches on the needle to begin the left shoulder panel (48 stitches).

Continue working back and forth on these 48 stitches in stockinette stitch until it measures the same length as the right shoulder panel.

Continue working this panel in stockinette stitch until it measures the same length as the right shoulder panel. End with a purl row.

Place both sets of shoulder stitches on separate circular needles (these can be a smaller size than the working needle).

Taking the size 11 circular needle, and starting with the left shoulder panel that you have just completed, knit 36 stitches.

The remaining 12 stitches of this panel are left on the holding needle.

Line up these 12 stitches with the first 12 stitches on the inside edge of the other shoulder panel. The panel with the working yarn is held on the outside, furthest from you, so that this overlap for the back of the tunic reverses direction, compared to the one you previously worked for the front.

Join the overlap by knitting through both stitches on the holding needles, turning two stitches into one on the working needle (see "Overlapping" on page 150 in the appendix). Then continue knitting the remaining stitches from the right shoulder panel.

After joining, you should have 84 stitches on the size 11 circular needle. Purl one row.

On the next knit row, begin the decrease section. You will decrease 5 stitches per row over each of the next 3 knit rows.

Decrease every 13th stitch, using SKP (slip 1, knit 1, pass slipped stitch over) for the first three decreases, k2tog for the last two decreases.

Purl 1 row.

Repeat these 2 rows, decreasing every 12th stitch on the second decrease row, and then every 11th stitch on the third decrease row.

You should have 69 stitches remaining.

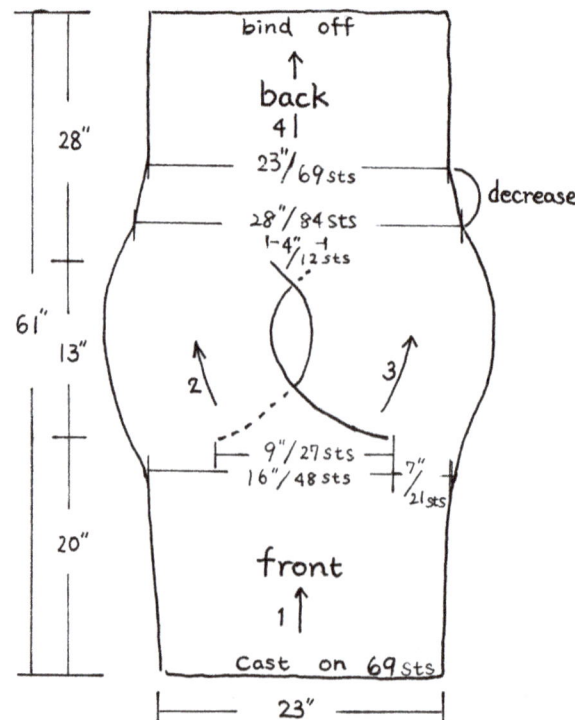

DIAGRAM 21

Continue working in stockinette stitch until the piece measures 28 inches from the back overlap.
Bind off all stitches.
Lay the tunic over a dress form or over the body, determine where the armhole opening should fall, and mark with a safety pin. Sew the front and back panels together along the side seams from this point to the bottom edge of the tunic.

Size Adjustment

Based on your gauge, cast on the number of stitches needed to give you the desired width for the front of the tunic. Use the diagram given as a template, and calculate the number of stitches that will belong to the back, front, and overlap/shoulder sections.

Overlap Shoulder Vest with Haramaki

Mikae Toma

Materials & Tools

Yarn: 8 oz, about 500 yds, worsted-weight wool/alpaca yarn

Needles: Circular knitting needle, size 10 1/2, 36 in. long; other needles for holding stitches (can be smaller size)

Gauge: 3 1/4 sts per inch

Color: A neutral or other single color

I used: Purplish brown, dyed with brazilwood and indigo, and lightly dipped into black walnut.

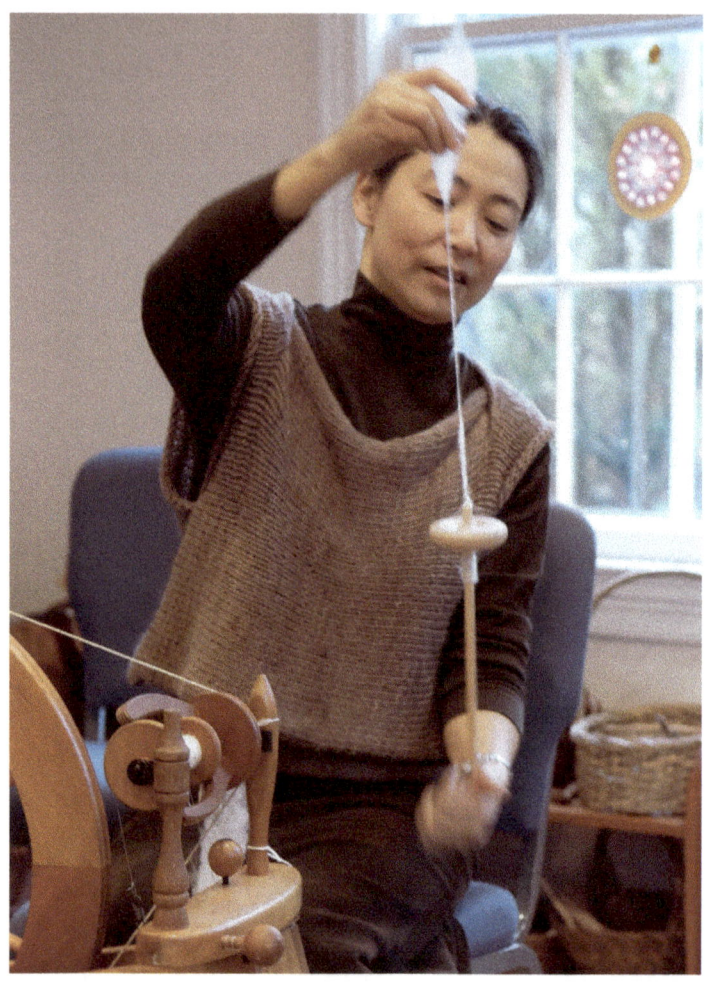

The overlaps of this piece support and reflect the movement of the shoulders.

The vest is knitted from side to side, beginning at one side edge, with the front and back as a single piece. After several rows, the stitches are divided, the front and back are knit separately, and then later they are reconnected. A matching piece, called a haramaki, adds extra warmth around the waist and brings a unique look to the vest.

This design was inspired by previous designs I had worked on, and arose in me through the work of my hands when creative new ideas flowed together with lingering images from previous designs.

As the drawing shows, this vest is simply made out of one piece worked in stockinette stitch from side to side. The back crosses over the front of the vest at the shoulders. As I was working, I found that the overlaps at the shoulders expressed the shape and movement of the shoulders in quite a remarkable way. When I wear this vest, it feels just right.

The characteristic roll of the stockinette fabric adds to the beauty of the design, as the inward-rolling edges bring a gentle roundness to the neckline. Making the front section wider than the back causes the vest to drape more deeply in the front due to the weight of the material.

When I was sewing the sides together, I realized that the bottom of this piece flared out a bit, since I made the front part wider than the back. It also was rather short, so it was especially important to match it with the right accompanying garment. Why not make something with the same yarn that would go with the piece? In this way, the idea of making a haramaki was born.

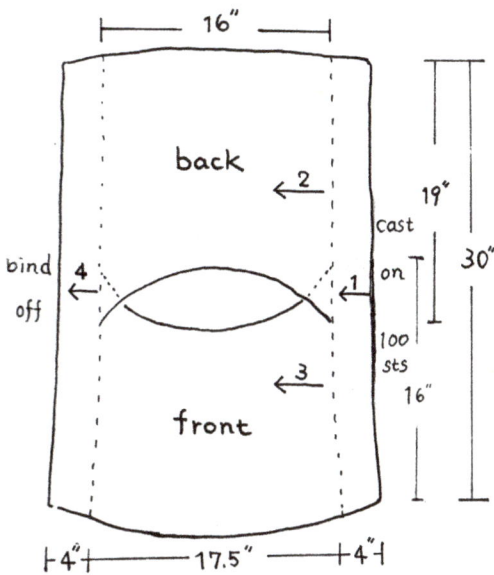

DIAGRAM 22

Instructions:

Make a swatch with the yarns, knitting needles, and stitches indicated. If necessary, adjust the needle size to obtain proper gauge (see "Making Swatches," page 45, and "Adjusting Sizes," page 47).

You will begin at one shoulder edge; cast on 100 stitches. Work stockinette stitch (knit one row, purl one row) until the piece measures 4 inches from cast-on edge.

On the next knit row, knit 62 stitches, then move the remaining 38 stitches to another needle or a string, holding them for later.

You will now be knitting the back of the vest. Continue to work stockinette stitch back and forth on 62 stitches until the piece measures 16 inches from the division point, ending with a purl row. Leave stitches on a circular needle or on a string.

Return to the 38 stitches you set aside. Turn the work so that you are starting on the purl side.

Purl 38 stitches, and then pick up and purl 10 more stitches from the reverse side of the back of the vest (see "Overlapping" on page 150 in the appendix). Turn the work and knit these 48 stitches to begin the front panel.

Continue working back and forth on these 48 stitches in stockinette stitch until this piece, the front of the vest, also measures 16 inches from the dividing point.

End with a purl row and break the yarn. Leave these stitches on the needle, or move them onto a smaller-sized needle.

Returning to the back panel, using the size 10 1/2 needle, knit 52 stitches. The remaining

10 stitches are left on the holding needle.
Line up these 10 stitches with the first 10 stitches on the neckline edge of the front panel. The panel with the working yarn is held on the outside, furthest from you, so that this overlap places the back panel on the outside of the garment, as with the other overlap. Join the overlap by knitting through both stitches on the holding needles, turning two stitches into one on the working needle (see "Overlapping" on page 150 in the appendix). Then continue knitting the remaining stitches from the front panel.
You should now have 100 stitches on the needle again.
Work across all stitches in stockinette stitch for 4 more inches.
Bind off all stitches.
Lay the tunic over a dress form or over the body, determine where the armhole opening should fall, and mark this point with a safety pin. Sew front and back panels together along the side seams from this point to the bottom edge of the vest.

Size Adjustment

Based on your gauge, cast on the number of stitches needed to give you the desired length for both front and back. Use the diagram given as a template, and calculate the number of stitches that will belong to the back, front, and overlap/shoulder sections, as well as how many rows to knit for the desired width of front and back sections. Remember that when knitting the front section, knitting more rows than for the back section will cause the front neck opening to drape a bit lower.

Matching Haramaki

Materials & Tools

Yarn: 2 1/4 oz, about 140 yds, of the same yarn as used for the matching vest

Needles: Straight or circular knitting needles, size 11 (or size needed to obtain gauge), either 13-inch straight needles or two 16-inch circular needles

Gauge: 3 sts per inch.

Traditionally, a haramaki is worn as an undergarment to bring warmth to the abdomen, but I designed it as an outer garment that brings warmth and adds beauty to the top.

This piece is knit lengthwise and is worn in such a way that the reverse stockinette section is folded over at the top to create a double layer.

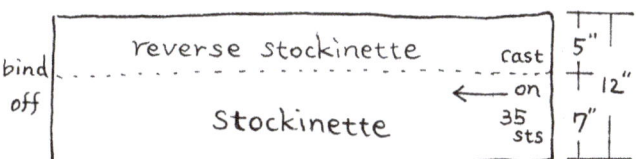

DIAGRAM 23

Instructions:

Cast on 35 stitches.
Row 1: Purl 15 stitches, knit 21 stitches.
Row 2: Purl 21 stitches, knit 15 stitches.
Repeat these 2 rows until the piece measures about 30 inches, or desired length from cast-on edge, to fit the wearer around the hip and waist area. Bind off all stitches. Sew cast-on edge to bound-off edge.

Overlap Shoulder Vest Variation
Mikae Toma

This tunic-like vest is somewhat longer and wider than the original vest.

I used two batches of yarns that were dyed with madder root and black walnut hulls. One batch was light and tended toward orange in color, and I used it mostly for the front section; the other was slightly darker and brownish, and I used it mostly for the back. I created a subtle gradation of color at the side panels.

Loose Tunic

Mikae Toma

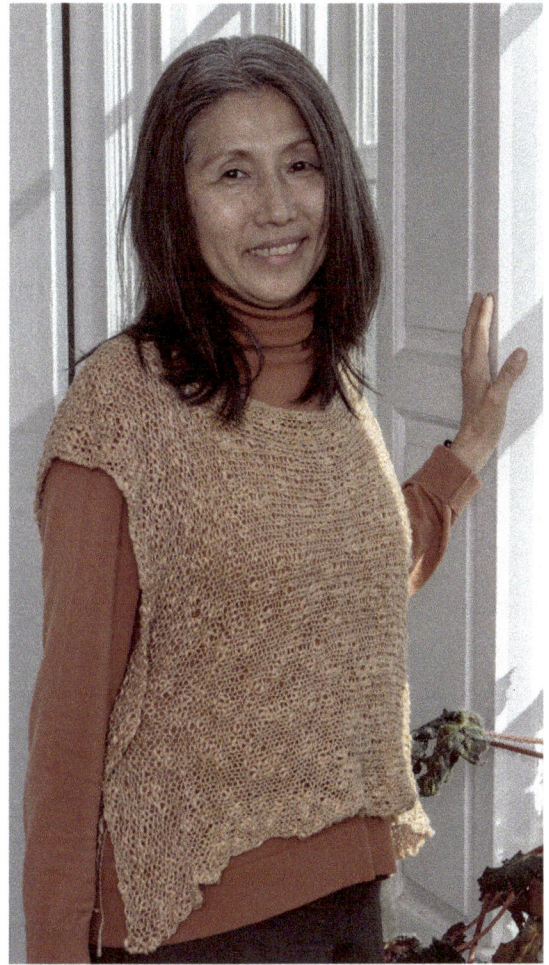

Materials & Tools

Yarn: 6 oz, about 500 yds, lightweight linen and cotton blend yarn, of a hand-spun quality

Needles: Circular knitting needle, size 10, 29 in. long; another circular needle for holding stitches (can be smaller size)

Gauge: 3 1/2 sts per inch

Color: A neutral or other single color

I used: Pinkish beige, dyed with cutch.

This tunic is modeled by our friend Miho. This piece is knitted lengthwise from side to side.

The conscious placement of purl rows within the overall stockinette texture brings different qualities to the various sections of the piece. The sides and back sections have garter stitch bands and purl stitch rows that increase in density toward the center of the back, and in the front the stockinette texture predominates.

One summer, while I was playing with the idea of creating a knitted piece using linen and cotton yarns, the picture of a light summer tunic that could be worn over a shirt arose in me. I created a good-sized sample swatch in stockinette stitch, using a lightweight linen and cotton blend, and found it was very intriguing to play with this swatch, imagining a way to make its characteristics come alive.

I observed with interest how the side edges of the stockinette fabric curled in naturally with the weight of this material. When I turned the piece ninety degrees, the grain of the stitches was horizontally aligned, and I thought the curled edge would be perfect for the front neckline. Making the front section slightly wider than the back would bring out the draping quality of the stockinette even more.

I thought the back section should be a little longer than the front, according to the shape of the body, and that the back section should look different from the front, for the back covers a flatter part of the body. It seemed right to have more vertical lines on the back, to emphasize the verticality of the spine. To reflect the movement of the shoulders and arms, I imagined a vertical emphasis, as well, in the shoulder area, but differing from the back. And I wanted the transition from the sides to the front section to be built gradually, rather than introducing a sudden change.

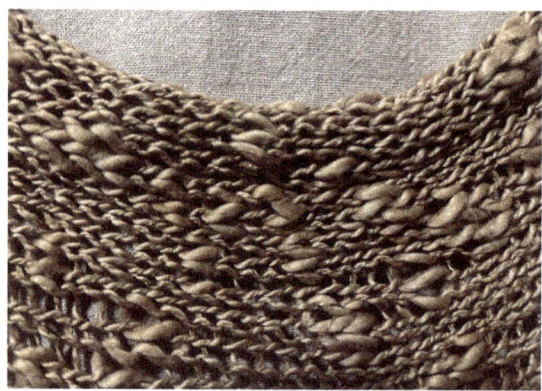

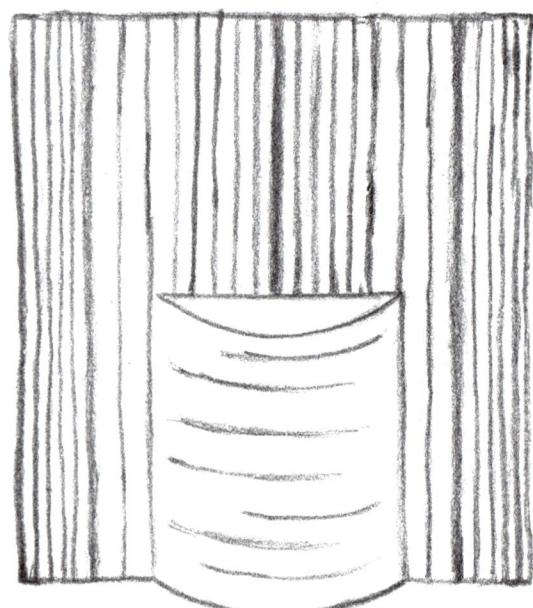

A design sketch for the Loose Tunic; the area in the center is the neck opening

Here is an outline drawing that shows the qualitative aspects of the design with its vertical and horizontal dimensions. To achieve this design, I played with rows of knit and purl stitches, keeping in mind the image I had drawn before I began with the knitting. As I knitted, I lived into the shapes, movements, and forces of our body, rather than simply trying to copy what I had intended. An exciting part of the creative process came when I progressed to the point where I could try the piece on, or put it over a dress form, to see the drape of the fabric and the overall design in three dimensions.

My original intention was not to sew the sides together, but to leave the edges unjoined below the arms, so the garment could be worn as a light summer poncho. However, at the same time I wanted to remain open, with an inner listening gesture, to what the piece wanted to become. It was very interesting that no matter how I looked, the piece seemed incomplete and awkward with its sides open. For several days I lived with the question of what to do, till I finally found a good way to make the sides move naturally with the arms by sewing a short seam a couple of inches in from the two edges.

It is always a question of how to come to a well-balanced, simple design with all the different parts integrated into an organic whole. By carrying the original image with an open mind, ready to welcome new ideas, we can immerse ourselves in a dynamic working gesture that is very satisfying.

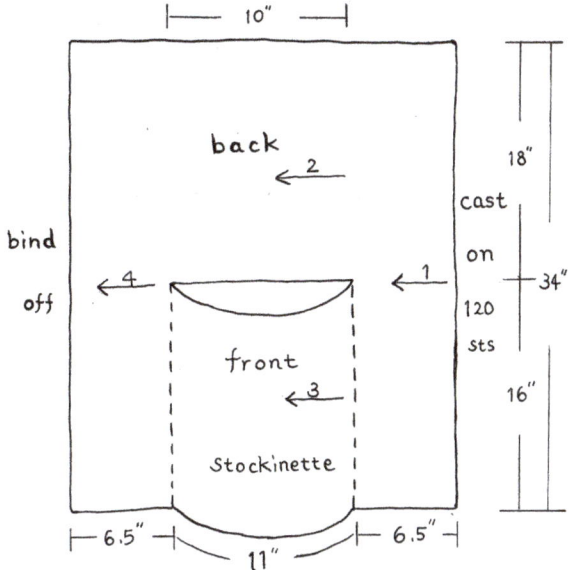

DIAGRAM 24

Instructions:

Make a swatch with the yarns, knitting needles, and stitches indicated. If necessary, adjust the needle size to obtain proper gauge (see "Making Swatches," page 45, and "Adjusting Sizes," page 47).

Exact instructions for textural changes are not given. Knitters are encouraged to make a swatch and plan their own design, playing with rows of knit and purl stitches for the sides and back of the poncho, with a progression toward the middle back that is then reversed on the other side. Making an outline drawing like the one above can be helpful.

The front panel is kept in stockinette stitch for a smooth texture.

Cast on 120 stitches. Work flat, varying knit and purl rows as desired.

When the piece measures 6 1/2 inches, begin the neckline division.

Work 64 stitches and place the remaining 56 stitches on a string or another circular needle to hold for later.

Continue working across the 64 stitches for the back, in your desired pattern of knit and purl rows, until the piece measures 5 inches from the neckline division—this is the center point of the back section.

Then begin reversing the pattern of knit and purl rows until the back section measures 10 inches total from the neckline division.

Leave these 64 stitches on a string or an extra circular needle and return to the 56 stitches set aside earlier.

Knitting all right-side rows and purling all wrong-side rows (stockinette stitch), work until this piece measures about 11 inches from the start of the stockinette section and can easily be joined with the 64 stitches from the back.

Join all stitches again on the long circular needle and continue working the stitch pattern for the second side section to mirror that of the first side.

When the second side measures 6 1/2 inches, bind off all stitches.

Place the tunic on a dress form or on the body and find a place under the arms where a short side seam will enhance its comfort and appearance.

Mark this place with a safety pin and sew a seam on each side.

Size Adjustment:

Use the diagram as a template to sketch out your own design. Numbers for the front and back sections can be adjusted according to your yarn, gauge, and desired length/width for the tunic.

Variation: Tunic Poncho
Mikae Toma

I worked this piece sideways, like the Loose Tunic (above, page 117), but with overlaps added at the shoulders, as with the Overlap Shoulder Vest (above, page 116).

Since the arms are covered only halfway, this poncho could be worn even in warm weather. It was knitted in a linen and cotton yarn, dyed a pinkish brown color with cutch.

An interesting aspect of this design is the change from purl to knit stitches in the same row. Since the number of knit stitches increases as the knitting gets closer to the neckline, a bias-like diagonal design arises.

To create your own design, work a swatch in which you play with this stitch pattern and decide how to use it on your garment.

On all right-side rows: knit.

On wrong-side rows, purl a certain number of stitches, then knit the rest of the row.

Increase and then decrease the number of purl stitches, creating a diagonal progression that is slightly zig-zag or staggered (see drawing).

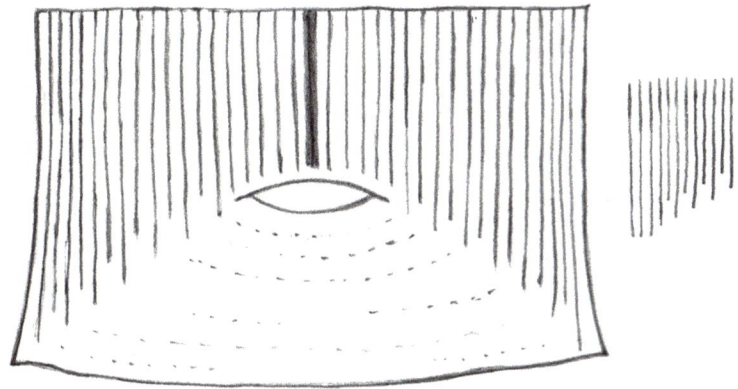

DIAGRAM 25

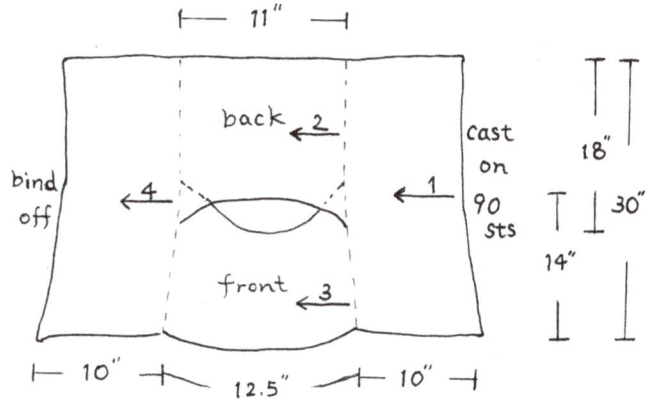

As in a true poncho, the sides are not sewn together, but stay open.

HORIZONTAL AND VERTICAL GESTURES: FROM SCARF TO JACKET

Bolero

Renate Hiller

Materials & Tools

Yarn: 6 oz, about 370 yds, worsted-weight alpaca/wool yarn; 6 oz, about 300 yds, of silk bouclé yarn

Needles: Circular knitting needles, size 10, 29 in. long

Gauge: 4 sts per inch

Color: Harmonizing shades of adjoining or complementary colors on the color wheel. The different types of yarn have a different main tone.

I used: Wool/alpaca yarn in greenish tones, dyed with yellow onion skins, indigo, and black walnut hulls; silk bouclé yarn in beige/rose tones dyed with red onion skins and black walnut hulls.

This bolero is knitted lengthwise, from side to side, in stockinette stitch, alternating two rows of alpaca/wool yarn with two rows of bouclé.

It can be worn in any season over a simple dress or blouse. The special quality and luster of the silk bouclé, as well as the wide dolman sleeves, bring a festive note to the piece. The bolero is reversible and can be worn either on the knit or purl side.

The word "bolero," with its three strong vowels, conjures up images of people dancing to beautiful music in Spain, in Cuba, and elsewhere—music that celebrates and expresses the joys and sufferings of life. The short jacket that we call a bolero may have its origin in the flamboyant outfits worn by dancers. I have spent much time in Spain and used to own a lovely bolero created by a Spanish designer, which inspired me to create this knitted garment.

My Spanish bolero was very lightweight, since the fabric was machine-knit with fine yarns. However, for my own design I pictured a warmer garment that had at the same time a lightweight quality. I also wanted to bring in a somewhat festive note. With these thoughts in mind, I knitted a swatch in stockinette stitch, alternating two rows of alpaca/wool yarn with two rows of silk bouclé. I made a larger swatch than usual—casting on 28 stitches and knitting 18 rows— because I wanted to see how the fabric would drape and how it would fall. The swatch also allowed me to figure out how many stitches I would need for a relatively wide sleeve. I opted for wide dolman sleeves to add to the festive quality of the bouclé yarn.

As I was knitting from one sleeve to the other across the body, I always pictured where on the body I was knitting. I also frequently "tried on" the piece by knitting to the middle of the needle and folding the piece in half. In this way, I could easily determine where on the body I was knitting and how I needed to shape the piece. This was how I determined how to make increases for the sleeves, cast on for the side seams, bind off and then on for the front edges, and how wide to make the back of the neck.

After I had knitted to the center of the piece (the middle of the back), I needed to make a mirror image for the other side. I had to cast on the right number of stitches for the front panel and decrease stitches to shape the arms, in exactly the same way I had increased on the other side.

After the final bind-off, it was a joy to sew the two short side seams on either side and try on the finished Bolero. It was lovely! All it needed was a bit of strengthening and shaping around the neck and front edges. I did this by embroidering two rows of chain stitches next to each other with the alpaca/wool yarn.

Essentially, I worked with two main colors: greenish tones in the wool/alpaca yarn to give a sense of foundation, and lighter beige/rose tones in the silk bouclé to bring playful airiness. I very consciously worked with the greenish tones, which are lighter at the edge of the sleeves, become darker around the shoulders, and then lighter again toward the head. I overdyed the finished piece in a light brazilwood bath to "warm up" all the shades.

The piece is reversible and can be worn either with the stockinette or the reverse stockinette side showing.

Instructions:

Make a swatch with the yarns, knitting needles, and stitches indicated. If necessary, adjust the needle size to obtain proper gauge (see "Making Swatches," page 45, and "Adjusting Sizes," page 47). If you use yarn in different shades, we recommend using the darker shades around the shoulders to indicate strength. Darker shades would also be suitable for the back of the piece.

With alpaca/wool yarn, cast on 56 stitches. Knit 1 row, purl 1 row.

Change to silk bouclé yarn and knit 1 row, purl 1 row.

Continue working in this way throughout the piece, carrying unused yarn along the side of the work.

To create the dolman shape of the sleeves, begin increasing in the 5th row, when knitting with the alpaca/wool yarn.

Increase 2 stitches every 5th row, 1 stitch at the beginning and 1 stitch at the end of the row. Continue with this rate of increase, making a total of 11 increase rows, for about 7 inches. For the second increase section, increase at the beginning and end of every second row (all the knit rows), 6 times, for about 4 inches.

This is the end of the sleeve section. The total number of stitches is now 90. Cut the silk bouclé yarn at the end of the last sleeve row where it is used.

Using the alpaca/wool yarn, cast on 12 stitches on both ends, using the backward-loop cast on over your thumb. Purl the next row, and cast on 12 stitches at the other end. The total number of stitches is now 114.

Knit the full length of the bolero (front and back), alternating both types of yarns as before, until the side section measures 7 inches.

To create the center back of the piece, bind off 57 stitches on the wrong-side row, then continue working back and forth on the remaining 57 stitches for 7 inches more.

On the next wrong-side row, cast on 57 stitches at the end of the row to create the

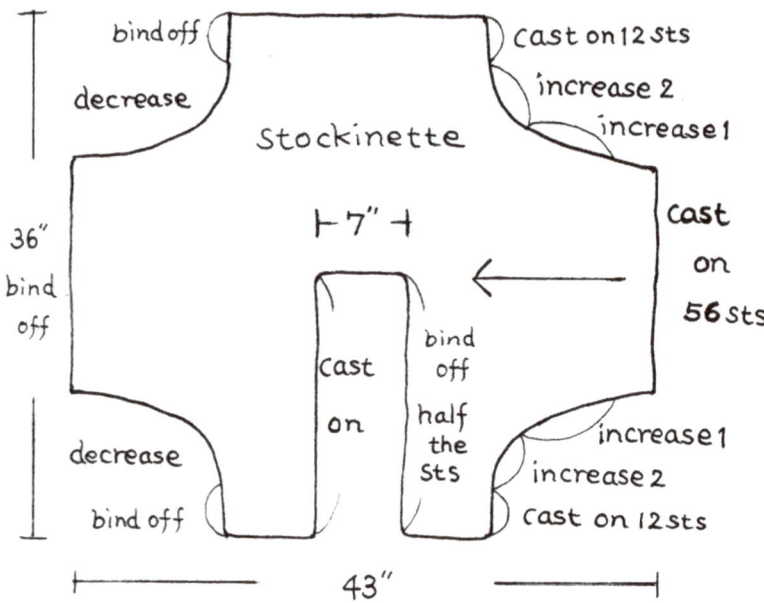

DIAGRAM 26

second side section.

Continue working as before until this section measures 7 inches.

For the second sleeve, create a mirror image of the first side by binding off 12 stitches on each side, then decrease 1 stitch on both sides of every knit row 6 times to mirror the increases on the other side, for about 4 inches of sleeve.

Switch to decreasing 1 stitch on each end of row every 5th row until the sleeve stitches are reduced to 56 again.

When sleeve length and width match that of the first sleeve, bind off all stitches.

Sew the seams under the arms to complete the piece.

You may strengthen and embellish the neck and side edges in the front by adding one or two rows of single crochet stitches, or embroider 2 rows of chain stitches.

Bolero Variation

For this variation, I followed the overall design of the original, but made the sleeves only five inches long, increasing stitches at the rate of the second increase section of the original bolero design. I used mohair bouclé yarn dyed a beige/golden hue with avocado pits and peels, and various tan/brownish wool yarns in matching light- to medium-dark tones, given by our friend Sono. I began with 70 stitches and knitted a narrow garter stitch band at the edge of the first sleeve, and later repeated it on the second sleeve. At the edges of the neck and the front openings, I knitted on a garter stitch band which ends with a rolled edge of 5 knit rows. I used the darkest colors of the wool yarns around the shoulder areas and in the center of the back, where I created a 5-inch–wide garter stitch band, alternating, as always, between the mohair and the wool yarns. The garter stitch band has, visually, a stronger linear quality than the overall piece, and the texture is a bit denser. This band is the back centerpiece of the bolero; it echoes the strength and verticality of the spine. I used 2 rows of crochet to close the side seams and make the bolero reversible.

Bolero Pullover Variation 1

When I tried on the Bolero and played with it, I put it on backwards (with the opening in the back) and really liked the look of it. So, the idea of this pullover was born.

The pullover is knit lengthwise from side to side, just like the Bolero, using the same materials in somewhat different shades. In a way, the pullover is easier to make than the Bolero, because you need to simply create an opening for the boat neck design. I have done this with shallow overlaps on either side of the neck (see "Overlapping" on page 150 in the appendix).

I worked the sleeve and first side section as for the Bolero. At the point where the neck opening needs to be made, to create the top layer of the overlap, I knitted to the middle of the piece, plus 3 stitches (a total of 60 stitches). I put the remaining stitches on a piece of yarn and knitted the back (about 12 inches wide). I then put these stitches on hold, returned to the reserved stitches, and knitted the front piece, picking up 6 stitches from the wrong side of the fabric, under the back overlap. I knitted the front of the sweater, making it somewhat wider than the back, for a lower neck opening in the front (4 to 8 rows more).

I joined the front and back together again, overlapping by 6 stitches, making sure the back overlap was on top of the front one.

I knitted the second side section to match the first, and then created a mirror image of the first sleeve.

After finishing the sweater, I decided to add the loosely falling collar. I picked up the stitches for the front and back sections separately, knit for about 1 inch, and then combined them by knitting in the round. I used the bouclé yarn only, working k1, p1 ribbing to make ridges that go well with the vertical design of the sweater. This is, of course, an optional addition. The overlap design is good both for strong corners and a loosely draping collar.

Bolero Pullover Variation 2

This striking variation of the Bolero Pullover was made and modeled by our friend Chris.

She followed the overall design of the Bolero Pullover Variation 1, but used a combination of wool yarns and mohair bouclé in somewhat different colors. The mossy green tones of the wool yarns converse beautifully with the gold tans of the mohair bouclé. She made the pullover slightly bigger by adding about one inch to the length of the body and two inches to the overall width. She left the soft contours of the boat neck opening and did not add a collar.

Hanten Jacket

Mikae Toma

Materials & Tools

Yarn: 22 oz, about 1,360 yds, worsted-weight yarn

Needles: Circular knitting needle, size 7, 47 in. long

Gauge: 5 sts per inch

Color: Dark to light shades of a single color

I used: Naturally shaded Jacob sheep's wool.

This piece came into existence because of my love for the wool from Jacob sheep.

All the single-ply yarns were handspun from roving of many different natural shades of gray, brown, and off-white.

The jacket has wide sleeves that create tremendous warmth and allow the arms to move freely inside.

The design was inspired by the traditional Japanese short winter coat called "hanten." A band knitted onto the front opening and around the neck brings extra warmth to these areas.

Instructions:

Make a swatch with the yarns, knitting needles, and stitches indicated. If necessary, adjust the needle size to obtain proper gauge (see "Making Swatches," page 45, and "Adjusting Sizes," page 47).

Color changes are made throughout the piece, grading from light to dark and back to light again. A front band is added in a medium shade. You may wish to draw a color diagram to plan out the transitions.

With the lightest shade of yarn, cast on 70 stitches.

Knit every row, increasing 1 stitch at the beginning of each row, until you have 190 stitches.

On the next two rows, cast on 40 stitches at the end of each row, for a total of 270 stitches.

Continue knitting every row until the piece measures 6 1/2 inches from these cast-on side edges.

At the beginning of the next row, bind off 140 stitches for the front edge, then continue knitting to the end of the row.

Knit back and forth on these stitches for another 7 inches. (The middle of this section will be the center back of the jacket, where you will begin to mirror the design and color changes.)

At the end of the next row, cast on 140 stitches. Create a mirror image of the first half of the garment:

Knit 6 1/2 inches.

Bind off 40 stitches at the beginning of the next two rows.

K2tog at the beginning of each subsequent row to decrease, until you have 70 stitches remaining.

Bind off all stitches.

To make the front band, with a long circular needle, starting at the bottom of the right side of the front opening, pick up and knit the stitches, going up along the front right edge, along the back of the neck, and down the left front edge. Knit back and forth until the band measures 4 inches. Bind off all stitches.

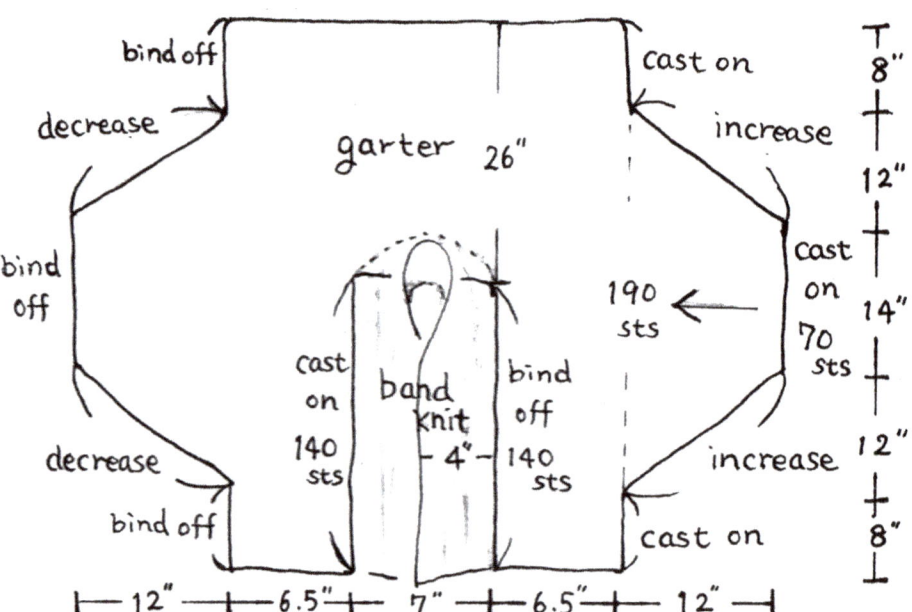

DIAGRAM 27

Part Three: Deepening Our Appreciation

Nature's Fibers: Wool, Silk, Cotton, and Linen

Wool and silk fibers are gifts from the world of animals, and cotton and linen fibers are derived from plants. These fibers have been used by human beings for millennia to create sheaths of beauty, warmth, and protection. A closer look at them cannot but fill us with awe and wonder.

These natural fibers are light and airy, and they have an affinity with the sun, absorbing light from it and growing toward it, in the case of plants, and even on the backs of animals. As these fibers come into being, they are part of delicate life processes. Wool fibers form a protective layer on the sheep's body; silk fibers, in the shape of a cocoon, are a shelter for the development of the silk moth; cotton fibers protect the seeds of the cotton plant; and linen fibers support the stem of the flax plant.

The domestication of animals and the cultivation of plants have been central human tasks since ancient times, and so have the manifold processes of transforming fibers to make items for daily use, like nets, ropes, cloth, and clothing. These activities—together with the building of shelters and the preparation of food—are closely intertwined with the story of human civilization. They formed the core of human practical activity until the beginnings of the Industrial Revolution.

Wool

Wool fibers are gifts from living, warm-blooded animals. Rams, ewes, and lambs share their coats with us, coats that protect them against cold, wind, rain, and snow, and shelter them from too much sun and heat.

Wool is a protein fiber created within the skin of the animal from modified body cells. Like human hair and skin, it contains silica, a conductor of sunlight. The longest and best fibers grow on the shoulders of the animal and can be up to twelve inches long. The fibers grow continuously, and sheep bred for wool are usually shorn once or twice a year. A merino sheep, with its fine wool, is protected by countless fibers, and the fleece can weigh as much as eighteen pounds.

When we see a whole fleece spread out before us after shearing, we are deeply moved by the beauty and softness of this gift, and we are glad to know that the sheep will soon grow another coat. The fibers smell "sheepy," and they feel warm and sticky to the touch. The stickiness is mostly due to the wool fat that lubricates the fibers and contains lanolin, a precious substance used in the cosmetics industry. When we separate a lock of fleece and hold it in our hands, we can see that the fibers are curly and are lying parallel to each other, cut ends and tips nicely aligned. When we separate one fiber from the rest, stretch it out and let it go, it springs back to its original form. We experience wool's great elasticity. When we glide with the thumb and index finger along the fiber in two different directions, we notice that in one direction it feels smooth and in the other it feels rough. What we experience as roughness are tiny scales on the surface of the fiber that overlap like the shingles on the roof of a house. They conduct the water away from the animal's skin. The scales are covered with an outer layer, similar to the substance of our fingernails, that repels water droplets but allows moisture in the form of steam or sweat to pass away from the body of the sheep—or that of the human being wearing a wool sweater.

The interior of each fiber, the cortex, is made up of countless spindle cells that are filled with air and are highly absorbent; in fact, wool can hold 40 percent of its weight in moisture without feeling wet to the touch, and then release the moisture through evaporation.

We wash our wool fibers in hot, soapy water to remove dirt and some of the wool fat, and we rinse them several times in clear water of the same temperature. After rolling the fibers in a towel to squeeze out some of the moisture, we leave them to dry outside in the shade, spread out on porous trays. Once this is done, the fibers are quite transformed, and we can appreciate their true coloring and loftiness. The fibers seem to bloom and shine—fine and medium wools have a delicate matte sheen, and long wools a beautiful luster. Clean wool fibers (with most of the wool fat removed) take dyes beautifully. In a hot dye bath, the fibers soak up the dyes till they become saturated with color. After rinsing and drying, the fibers sparkle with new life.

Articles of clothing made of wool surround us with pleasant warmth, are elastic, have a wonderful drape, and are practically wrinkle-free. They provide us with layers of comfort and beauty, and they foster our well-being.

Today, many other animal fibers from all over the world are at our disposal. They can come from the Andean camel family: alpaca, llama, guanaco, and vicuña; the Saharan and Asian camels; the cashmere and Angora goats; the Central Asian yak; and the Angora rabbits that can live almost anywhere.

Silk

Silk threads are a gift from an insect, the silk moth. The life cycle of the silk moth is one of continuous metamorphosis. Tiny eggs laid by an adult moth are the first manifestation of new life. Soon, hungry caterpillars emerge and voraciously devour large quantities of leaves. They grow so rapidly that they need to molt (shed their skin) four times within one month. After this period of rapid growth, they stop eating and begin to spin threads around themselves. As the double threads emerge from the two spinnerets (glands) located in their heads, they follow the light of the sun to form a cocoon. This cocoon is the protective space the animal needs for its further development from pupa to moth. After the moth emerges from the cocoon, it mates, lays eggs, and soon dies.

The luster of fine silk fabric seems to speak of the caterpillar's affinity to the light of the sun. In the dyeing process, silk fibers absorb color instantaneously and shimmer like the wings of a butterfly in the summer sun.

Silk, a protein fiber, is the strongest natural fiber for its weight. It is porous, resists mold and mildew, and can absorb 30 percent of its weight in moisture without feeling damp. In spite of its light weight, silk provides pleasant warmth. Silk is also elastic and resilient; it can stretch 20 percent without breaking and will spring back to its original form.

Although there are several types of silk moths living in the wild, the Chinese tussah being the best known among them, most silk produced today comes from the cultivation of the species *Bombyx mori*. It was originally found in China, and is now mainly bred in China and India. In sericulture, the life cycle of the animal is interrupted by heat at the pupa stage, since the adult moth, in order to emerge from the cocoon, would make a hole and thus ruin the continuous thread. For reeling (unwinding) the threads, the cocoons are soaked in hot water to remove some of the sericin, the sticky substance that holds the threads together. Several cocoon threads are then reeled together to make one fine silk thread. The threads forming one cocoon are about one mile long and have to be unwound carefully. About two thousand cocoons are needed to weave enough silk for one dress.

So-called peace or ahimsa silk is made without interrupting the life cycle of the insect in the pupa stage. The moth is allowed to mature and leave the cocoon by making a hole. Her adult life seems geared toward propagation; she flies off and soon mates, lays hundreds of eggs, and dies. The hole in the cocoon results in shorter fibers and requires spinning, rather than the usual process of reeling together the long fibers from several cocoons.

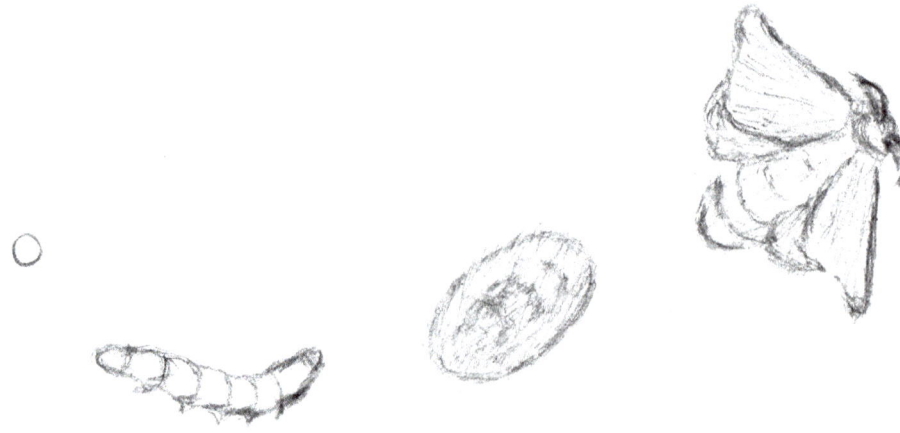

Silk fibers, intended by nature to provide a sheltered space for delicate life processes to occur, can serve as ideal material for beautiful and healing layers of clothing. As we benefit from these fibers, let us be conscious of the gifts bestowed by this insect with its amazing life cycle, and let us be grateful for the patient and painstaking labor of many skilled workers.

Cotton

Cotton fibers are gifts from growing plants. The short, soft fibers surround and protect several seeds held together in a kind of pod, called a boll. Cotton plants belong to the mallow or malva family of plants, which include many edible and medicinal varieties. They grow in tropical and subtropical climates in many parts of the world. It is quite amazing to experience the growing process of this plant. With a houseplant growing indoors, or maybe on a balcony or terrace, we can observe with wonder how the drop-shaped seed grows and develops into a lovely flowering seed- and cotton-bearing plant, all within a relatively short time, from spring to fall.

As the plant grows, the leaves grow larger and change their shapes, from one point in the beginning to three points and five points later on. Between the main stem and the leaf stems of the plant, buds appear, encased by three fuzzy leaf-like coverings that soon open up to allow the growth of a beautiful flower. This flower is self-pollinating. The color of the flower is pure white on the first day, turns pinkish on the second through third day, and then withers and drops off, revealing the beginning stages of the boll. The boll then grows larger and larger, till approximately the size of a walnut. At this stage, it slowly dries and then splits open into four sections, revealing a bit of its fiber treasure inside. Later, as the boll bursts open completely, the fibers become fluffy and are held by a shiny golden hull that is a bit prickly. This cotton boll contains hundreds of thousands of fibers as well as many seeds.

Cotton is a cellulose fiber with a staple length of one-half to two inches. The fibers feel very soft to the touch and are highly absorbent. They become about 30 percent stronger when they are wet, and they can be boiled in the washing process without damage. This makes cotton an ideal material for underwear, bedding, shirts, blouses, napkins, and the like. When hand-spinning cotton, it is advisable to add a good amount of twist in order to make the short fibers hold well together and to prevent them from pilling. The delicate, short fibers can even be turned into strong ropes by adding a good amount of twist in the spinning process and by plying several spun strands together.

Cotton plants

Today, cotton is the most used natural fiber in the world. India, the United States, and China are the largest producers. Worldwide, the cultivation of cotton depends largely on chemical fertilizers and pesticides, and in the last decades, genetic modification has become widespread. Rising concerns about the damage inflicted on the natural environment and to human health has led to the growth of organic cotton farming and processing.
As concerned citizens of the world, we can make a difference by purchasing items made with organic cotton fibers, and we should never forget the enslavement of many people that forms part of the history of the cultivation and production of this precious material.

Linen

Linen fibers are gifts from the flax plant, one of the oldest agricultural crops. Linen fibers are so-called bast fibers, since they form part of the stem of the plant as a kind of inner skin. Other bast fibers are produced from hemp, ramie, jute, and kenaf; and from wild plants, including nettle, kudzu, wisteria, and paper mulberry. (They are distinguished from leaf fibers, such as abaca, raffia, sisal, etc.) The processes involved in separating fibers of the flax plant from the other materials of the stems may seem laborious, but the fibers are much valued for their exceptional qualities and their durability.

The Latin name of the flax plant is *Linum usitatissimum,* with the second part of the name meaning "most useful." This plant is most useful indeed, since it not only supplies us with lustrous linen fibers, but also with oil-rich seeds, which are used as food and medicine and are pressed to make nutritious linseed oils. Flax plants like a cool climate and a rich soil. They are grown in full sun and are seeded densely, so that they will support each other while they grow to a height of about three to four feet. The individual plant, with its slender growth and small, slender leaves, has a strong vertical quality and seems to stretch towards the sun. A whole flax field in bloom is a delight to see, as the lovely blue flowers seem to mirror the color of the sky. Their color is fleeting, however, since the flowers' five petals open before noon and then fall to the ground later the same day. After the petals have fallen, the carpel quickly grows and forms into a pea-sized boll. During harvesting time, which can happen about a hundred days after the sowing, the plants are pulled out of the ground with their short roots intact. Then comes a time of resting in the fields, exposed to rain and sun, while the process called "retting" occurs: microorganisms help the fibers to loosen their bond with the inner core and outer bark layer of the plant stalks.

The dry plants are then brought into the barn or factory and go through a number of processes to free the fibers from the rest of the plant matter. First, the seeds are separated out through the process of rippling, and after the seeds have been separated, the plant stalks are more or less beaten (breaking, scutching, hackling are terms used for this process), and combed to separate the chaff as well as the short fibers, called tow, from the long fibers. This was once a laborious process, but is fully mechanized today in the halls of large factories.

Flowering flax plants

Linen is a cellulose fiber with a high wax content, which gives it its luster and special beauty. The fibers extend along the whole length of the plant. They are strong, soft, and lightweight, and feel smooth and cool to the touch. The fibers repel moisture when it first touches them, but then absorb it slowly, and, under the right conditions, dry very fast. For spinning the linen fibers by hand, a distaff is a good tool to use. It holds the long fibers in place, while some of them are drawn out of the fiber mass. Often, the fibers are lightly moistened to help the spinning process and give the fibers a smooth appearance.

When woven, washed, and ironed, there is a freshness and crisp appearance to linen that is unparalleled by any other fiber. A linen dress or shirt keeps us cool in the summer and can be washed countless times without losing its special characteristics of smoothness, strength, and durability—characteristics that have been appreciated by painters for centuries.

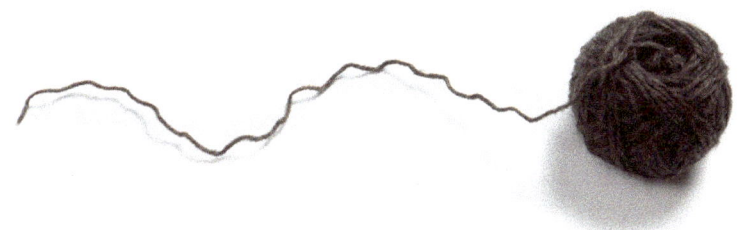

The Gestures and Tools of Hand-Spinning: Stick, Stone, Spindle, and Wheel

I see God in every thread that I draw on the spinning wheel.

—Mahatma Gandhi

For every revolution of the wheel spins peace, goodwill, and love.

—Mahatma Gandhi

The transformative powers of spinning and weaving are mirrored in the mythology and fairy tales of many cultures. In the fairy tale "Spindle, Shuttle, and Needle," from the German collection of the Brothers Grimm, the poor girl who diligently spins, weaves, and sews with the blessings of her godmother becomes a queen.

Plato, in *The Republic*, compared the shaft of the spindle to the axis of the universe and the whorl to the revolving starry heavens. We modern human beings may be able to tune into the cosmic dimensions when we observe the drop spindle spinning on its axis, like our planet Earth, and the loose fibers spiraling into form.

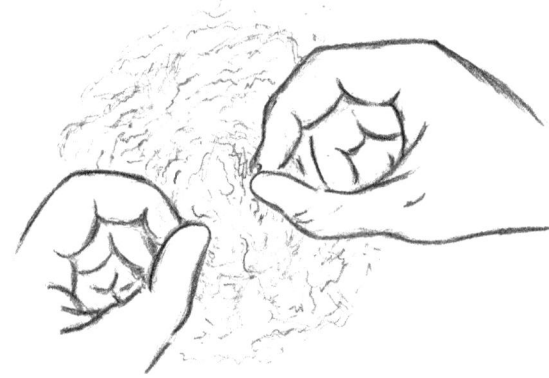

On a practical level, learning to spin can be a journey of discovery full of good challenges and joys. It encompasses learning about various sheep breeds and the special qualities of their fibers, as well as getting acquainted with different tools that have served people all over the world for thousands of years and are still being used today.

These spinning tools can be as simple as a small section of a twig used for spinning on the thigh or a stone and stick tied together with a piece of yarn used as a drop spindle. However, most spindles are constructed in such a way that a straight shaft goes through the center of a disk or large bead, called a spindle whorl. The whorl gives weight to the spindle and adds momentum as the spindle is turning. With this type of spindle, the spun yarn is wound along the shaft, spiraling upward and downward in an orderly fashion.

No matter what tool we plan to use for hand-spinning, whether a spindle or spinning wheel, the preparatory processes begin with the careful washing and drying of a fleece. (In rare cases, if a fleece is very clean, we can spin it "in the grease" without washing.) After the fleece is dry, we begin by pulling a lock from the fleece and we loosen the fibers of this lock with our fingertips, a process called "teasing." Depending on the type of yarn we hope to create, the process of loosening can be augmented by activities that align the fibers and remove short fibers from the fiber mass through the use of combs, hand carders, or a drum carder. The actual process of spinning begins when we hold a mass of fiber in one hand, pull out a bunch of fibers from this mass, and feed it into the spiraling motion created by the spindle or the wheel.

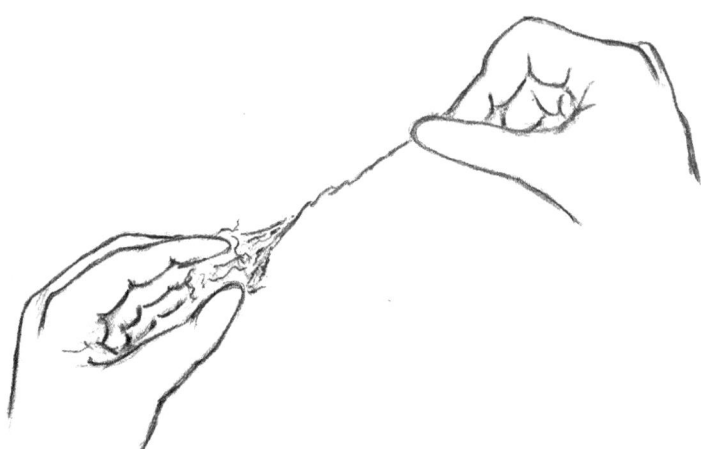

Spinning fibers with the fingertips

THE GESTURES AND TOOLS OF HAND SPINNING

The playful and gentle working with the fibers not only reveals their special qualities to all our senses, it also helps us to enter a space of inner calm. Our hands become warmer, and our breathing tends to deepen. The rhythmic work gestures, in harmony with the turning of the spindle or the wheel, unfailingly engender an experience of centeredness.

Spinning with a stone and stick spindle

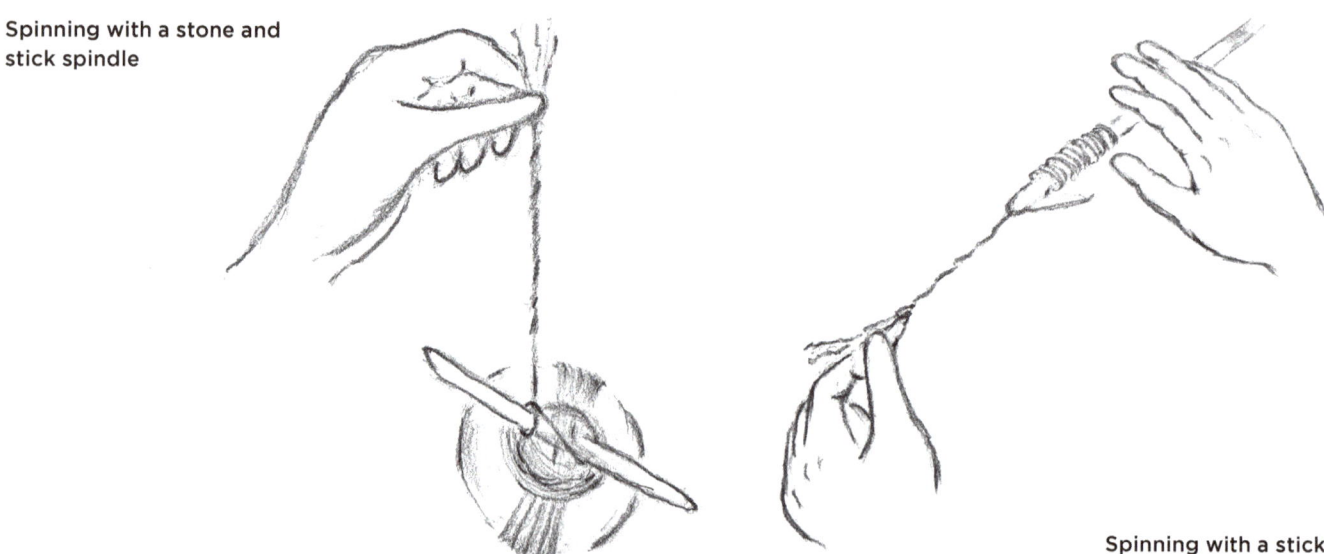

Spinning with a stick

When it is time to remove the spun yarn from the spindle shaft or the bobbin of the wheel to create a skein of yarn, we are always amazed at the magical process we have been involved in. The short fibers of the fleece have been transformed into a beautiful and lively yarn. The skein in our hands is the result of hours of careful and devoted work and will be turned into a treasured piece of knitting. The garments featured in this book that we have made with our hand-spun yarns have a special place in our heart.

With a rotating spindle in our hands, it is astonishing to think that we are practicing the skills handed down to us from generations of spinners, and that we are using a tool that stands at the beginnings of human civilization.

A basket of wool locks and simple spinning tools gathered in nature

Spinning with the drop spindle

THE GESTURES AND TOOLS OF HAND SPINNING

The Magic of Color and the Process of Dyeing with Plants

Colour is to the spiritual life what food and air and water are to the physical life. As these nourish our bodies, so colour nourishes the soul and spirit.

—Gladys Mayer, *Colour, Healing, and the Human Soul*

As we awaken in the morning and open our eyes, a world of color greets us and accompanies us throughout the day till we close our eyes again and go to sleep. From sunrise to sunset, we are embedded in a sea of color, shining and glittering with many hues. The sky and clouds above us, the grass, the flowers and trees, the birds and butterflies—all are ready to delight us with their display.

Nature's colors are never fixed and monotone, but interweave many hues in the ever-changing atmosphere of darkness and light. The appearance of a rainbow in the sky may bring tears to our eyes, as the gentle colors resonate in us and the doors to the heavens seem to open for a precious moment in time.

Colors are all around us, whether conjured by nature or by human striving. Through the ages, human beings sought to adorn themselves with color and surround themselves with colorful objects in their homes and places of worship. Minerals, plants, and animals supplied what was needed to satisfy this quest, and many hours of human labor were devoted to making the colors available for use in inks, dyes, and paints. Beautiful clothing, paintings, and artifacts were the result of this tremendous labor.

At the end of the nineteenth century and moving into the twentieth, a new era came into being as the chemical industry managed to create dyes and pigments synthetically, using coal tar and, later, petroleum as the primary substance for all colors. With the development of mass production, an endless array of objects saturated with color became available for daily use and flooded the market. Never before had colored objects been so ubiquitous and so easily obtainable. Today, we have become so used to our colorful surroundings that we take them for granted and are in danger of not truly seeing them anymore.

In order to experience the inner forces and universal qualities of a color, we need to put aside our personal likes and dislikes and, with our full attention, try to really see and "listen." Then the color may begin to "speak" to us in an objective way, revealing its qualities, its special language. According to its nature, each color may touch us in a particular way. It may speak loudly or softly; it may seem to come toward us or invite us to follow; it may seem warm or cool, festive or joyous. A room festively decorated in red may lift our spirits and invite us to dance, while a blue room may have a calming effect.

Like a circle of good friends, the colors form intimate relationships with each other. Looking at a color circle, we encounter the primary colors of red, blue, and yellow. When a primary color unites with one of its neighbors, a secondary color arises. From red and blue, purple arises; red and yellow together form orange; blue and yellow form green. Mixed in varying degrees, an infinite array of hues is created. In this way, while painting or dyeing fibers we can create a whole color circle just by working with the three primary colors.

When observing color combinations, we may experience harmony or disharmony; some colors may "sing" together, others may practically fight with each other. We experience colors next to each other and colors opposite each other in the color circle as harmonious. The complementary colors—those that are opposite each other in the color circle (red and green, purple and yellow, blue and orange)—strike us as the most complete, since they lead us back to the basic triad of the primary colors. Each color can call forth in us its complementary color: if we focus, for example, on a single patch of blue for a short while and then move our gaze to a white surface, the complementary color—a delicate, shimmering orange—will arise as an after-image. In this way, the wholeness of the triad of primary colors is created by our organism.

In search of color for our yarns and garments, we made a conscious decision to use dyes derived from plants. When we observe the many colors in a flower garden, we are struck by their beauty and their special harmony. The colors in the plant kingdom are created by the sun—they are a gift from the sun. When these colors unite with the fibers in the dye process, their beauty may be preserved for a long time. Take as an example the oldest known textile decorated with indigo blue, found in Huaca, Peru; it is 6,200 years old. Each color carried by the fibers derives its character from one individual plant or from several plants. The colors somehow seem to be alive, and they strike us with their special beauty and luminosity. Like the flowers in the garden, they always harmonize—they never clash or "bite" each other. Colors derived from plants are never one-sided, since each one of them carries a symphony of secondary tones within it. These living colors are a therapy for the senses, and they bring nourishment to our soul, when we work with them or perceive them in our environment. Even when applied to fibers, plant colors seem to still be alive, and when they eventually fade, they do so gracefully.

In our hands-on work, we gathered plant materials in the gardens and in the local countryside. We dug up roots of the madder plant, gathered the flowers of dyer's chamomile, yellow cosmos, and coreopsis, and harvested whole weld and Japanese indigo plants. The collection of black walnuts and acorns in the fall became an important part of the rhythm of the year. While tending the dye garden, with its perennial and annual plants, through the seasons, we learned to "know their ways" and unlock some of their secrets: who would think that the modest-looking madder plant, "crawling" on the ground with its prickly leaves and tiny yellowish flowers, would carry a beautiful red color in its brown roots? Who would think that the green leaves of indigo could become the source of heavenly blues?

In addition to the gifts from local plants, we also obtained gifts from different regions of the world: brazilwood and Osage orange in the form of wood chips, and cutch and indigo as dye concentrates. These precious materials connected us to faraway lands, and to cultures different from our own.

Sun dye jars lined up on a garden wall at the Fiber Craft Studio. As the sun warms the water, the fibers absorb the colors from the plants.

After gathering and preparing the plants, the actual process of dyeing begins. Immersed and soaked in water—with the help of warmth captured outside from the sun or inside on a stove —the plants part with their colors; the colors become liberated from the plant substances and are carried by the water. This beautifully colored water, the dye bath, then becomes the source of color for the fibers. While immersed in the dye bath, the colors unite with the fibers, often with the aid of a metallic salt called a mordant.

As we become actively engaged in these processes, working in intuitive ways with each plant, magic seems to happen. Like the alchemists of medieval times, we are engaged in working with the four elements of nature—earth, water, air, and fire or warmth—to produce processes of transformation that deeply touch us and lead to amazing results. Inspired by the past, we are consciously performing deeds of the future, using renewable resources and human striving to bring healing impulses into the culture of our time.

Mikae harvesting yellow cosmos in the dye garden.

Harvesting Dyer's Chamomile

A Fall harvest basket full of treasures: Coreopsis flowers and black walnuts

THE MAGIC OF COLOR

Plant Metamorphosis, courtesy Peter Wolf

Concluding Thoughts

The creation of *Knitting by Heart* has been an enriching journey of transformation.

May the seeds we have sown on this journey grow into the future and bring impulses of renewal to the art and craft of making clothing.

Clothing . . .

that acknowledges and fosters our true humanity—our physical as well as our soul-spiritual nature and well-being;

that is universal and individual; that fits into our time and is timeless; that is practical, functional and beautiful;

that is lovingly made by hand with gratitude for nature's gifts in our hearts and the health of our planet Earth in mind.

—Renate Hiller

In creating *Knitting by Heart,* we have come to this way of working through our own journey.

It has been a life-bringing journey for us, with a growing awareness of its healing potential.

When we transform gifts from nature, we ourselves are transformed.

Recognizing essential qualities in things as we strive for truth, beauty, and goodness leads to a path of creation, a path to becoming true human beings.

Weaving together thinking, feeling, and willing in the process of creation engenders harmony within ourselves, which in turn brings harmony to our surroundings.

As our journey on this path continues to evolve, we hope it will give rise to a sense of community and a spirit of service among our fellow travelers.

—Mikae Toma

Acknowledgments

Looking back at the creation of this book and the research that flowed into it, we are filled with deep gratitude. During the book's lengthy gestation, we have been encouraged and helped by many individuals who have been by our side. From the early stages of writing to the final manuscript, family members, students, and friends and colleagues from the Fiber Craft Studio have been most supportive. Their interest and their belief in the importance of this project has been unwavering and has meant a great deal to us.

In the early stages of manuscript writing, we were supported by several friends and experienced Waldorf educators, who shared their insights and recommendations with us. Very special thanks go to: Brigitte Bley-Swinston, Michael Howard, and Giannina Zlatar and Jaime Arenas.

Melanie Falick, well-known writer, editor, and creative consultant, author of *Making a Life: Working by Hand and Discovering the Life You Are Meant to Live* (Artisan 2019), graciously consulted with us on the manuscript. Her interest in *Knitting by Heart* and her continued support have been a major gift.

Lory Widmer Hess, long-time friend, experienced editor and writer, author of *When Fragments Make a Whole* (Floris Books 2024), and graduate of the Fiber Craft Studio Sheep to Shawl program, entered the manuscript development in its later stages and took on the writing of sample instructions as well as further editing of the manuscript. We have been blessed by her enthusiasm for *Knitting by Heart* and her dedication to bringing the manuscript to its completion.

Our project manager Donna Miele, who also picked up the post-developmental editing, and Claudio Rodriguez, our excellent photographer and designer, worked in tandem to support and guide us in the self-publishing process, making this seemingly daunting task into a creative endeavor. Thank you to our Kickstarter supporters and other generous donors, without whom self-publishing would not have been financially possible. Thank you also to our proofreaders, members of the Fellowship Community in Chestnut Ridge, New York, for polishing this rather involved text.

Fiber Craft Studio friends Janet Gómez, Chris Marlow, Laura Montano, Miho Suzuki, and Sono Kuwayama supported Renate in her task to reknit some of the sample projects that were lost in the fire at Pine Lodge. They not only created beautiful variations in the spirit of research but also acted as models for the photography. Their enthusiasm and goodwill turned a tragedy into a gift.

Much appreciation goes to photographer Lisa Kachajian, who provided the photographs © 2025 on pages 15 (right-side), 64 (top), and 75, and, in the spirit of friendship, collaborated with Renate during her initial explorations for the book's photography. For more information, visit www.lisakachajian.com.

Our book has been enhanced and its content deepened by the color circle painted by Brigitte Bley-Swinston, which appears on page 143 in "The Magic of Color and the Process of Dyeing with Plants," and the drawing *Plant Metamorphosis* by Peter Wolf, which appears on page 146, to accompany "Concluding Thoughts."

With much appreciation and deep gratitude, Renate Hiller and Mikae Toma

APPENDIX

Techniques

Provisional cast-on:

Using an extra piece of yarn, make a slip knot and place it onto a crochet hook.

Hold your crochet hook in your right hand and a knitting needle in your left hand. With the long tail of the yarn behind the needle, cross the crochet hook in front of the needle and wrap the yarn behind the needle.

Draw the yarn through the slip knot. Now there is one stitch cast on the needle.

Position the yarn behind the needle before making the next stitch. Repeat wrap and draw to create the desired number of stitches.

To finish casting on, simply make a couple of the chain stitches and cut the yarn, then pull the yarn through the loop.

Removing the provisional cast-on and picking stitches up to knit in the opposite direction:

At the end of the provisional cast-on, draw the yarn back through the loop and undo the extra chain stitches. Then, as you carefully unravel the provisional cast-on one stitch at a time, place the "live" stitches on a working needle.

At the very end, there will be a half stitch left since the stitches have become upside down. Count the stitches and adjust to the desired number by picking up or dropping the half stitch.

Increases

Make a yarn over (YO). This will create a hole where the increase was made.

Knit into front and back (K1F&B). Knit into the front side of a stitch as usual, and leave it on the needle. Then knit into the remaining back side of the same stitch and slip it off onto the right needle.

Make One increase (M1), right (R) and left (L); make a symmetrical pair. Make One left (M1L): With the left needle, lift the yarn between two stitches of the previous row, inserting your needle from front to back. Then knit into the loop through the back. Make One right (M1R): With the left needle, lift the yarn between two stitches of the previous row from back to front. Then knit into the loop through the front.

Decreases

Knit two together (k2tog). Treat two stitches as one the usual knit way. This decrease leans to the RIGHT.

To make a symmetrical pair, use **Slip, Slip, Knit (SSK),** originally by Barbara Walker. Slip the first and second stitches knitwise, one at a time, then insert the tip of the left-hand needle in front of these two stitches from the left and knit them together from this position (quoted from Elizabeth Zimmermann, *Knitting Without Tears* [Scribner, 1971]). This decrease leans to the LEFT.

Overlapping

Picking up the stitches on the reverse stockinette side:

Pick up the number of stitches as indicated and work with the new yarn as instructed.

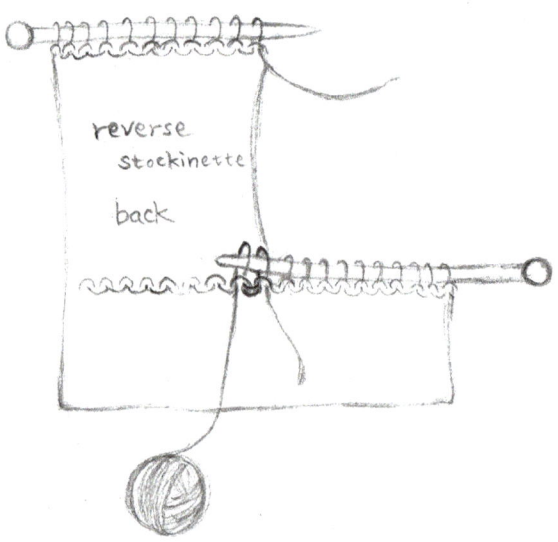

Joining the overlap:

Knit through both stitches on the holding needles to turn two stitches into one on the working needle.

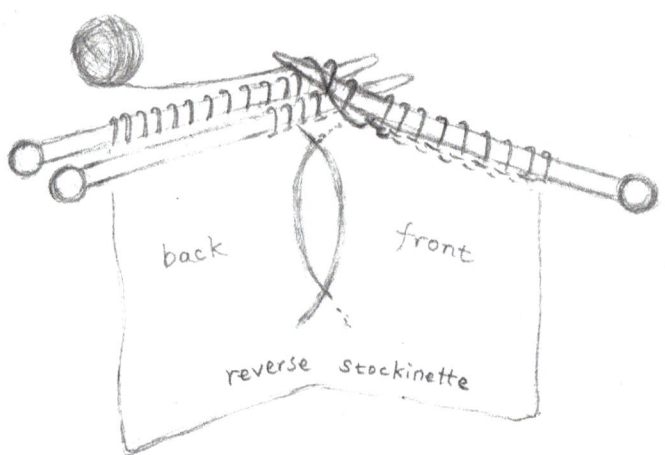

On Blocking and Caring for Your Woolen Knits

With the right treatment, your woolen treasure can last a lifetime. The final shaping after the knitting can be accomplished by the process called "blocking." When wool is damp, it can be coaxed into shape by gentle pulling, pushing, and stretching, and it will keep this shape when it is dry. For this purpose, a blocking board could be used, but this is not necessary for our simple designs. The knitting can simply be laid out on a towel dampened with a spray bottle and shaped, or it can be soaked in a lukewarm soap bath. We like to use a no-rinse soap, like Eucalan, for this purpose. A fifteen-minute bath not only cleans, but also reconditions the fibers with lanolin and essential oils.

Be aware that wet wool needs careful handling to avoid felting, overstretching, or both. Lift the knitting from the bath with the help of a colander and let the water drip for a while before rolling the piece in a towel to absorb most of the moisture. After the final shaping let the knitting dry completely and store it in a drawer or in the closet, protected by a pillowcase. Moth larvae do not eat through woven cotton cloth, and the cloth (rather than a plastic bag) allows the piece to breathe.

Sources for Materials

Most of the yarns for the projects in this book have come from Henry's Attic in Monroe, New York. Henry's Attic offers a wide variety of high-quality natural fibers and undyed yarns from all over the world (www.hayarns.com).

Lamb's Pride yarns, 85 percent wool and 15 percent mohair, have come from the Brown Sheep Company, a family-owned mill in Nebraska (brownsheep.com).

We have also sourced fleeces and yarns directly from farms connected to the Fibershed movement of farmers and makers that seek to foster a local, human- and earth-centered textile economy. Visit fibershed.org for more information.

- Jacob wool fleeces from Jenny Jump Farm in Northern New Jersey. The farm is a member of the New Jersey Fibershed. Visit them at jennyjumpfarm.com.
- Clare's Corrie Yarn (72% Corriedale, 28% Wensleydale) from Foster Sheep Farm in upstate New York. The farm is connected with the Fibershed movement via the Hudson Valley Textile Project. Visit them at fostersheepfarm.com.
- Elderlana Merino from Fox Fiber–Vreseis Ltd., owned by Sally Fox. The farm grows mostly colored cotton and is connected to the California Fibershed. Visit them at vreseis.com.

In addition, Mikae sourced some fleeces and yarns in Japan.

Recommended Resources for Reading, Study, and Practice

For additional inspiration and help with knitting projects, we recommend two classic books: *Knitting from the Top* by Barbara G. Walker (Charles Scribner's Sons, 1972) and *Knitting Without Tears* by Elizabeth Zimmermann (Simon and Schuster, 1971). Both books are available through the used books market.

For starting a dye garden, we used Rita Buchanan's *A Dyer's Garden*, published in 1995 by Interweave Press, which seems to be out of print.

For plant dyeing we recommend *Wild Color* by Jenny Dean and Karen Diadick Casselman (Potter Craft, 2010) and *Harvesting Color: How to Find Plants and Make Natural Dyes* by Rebecca Burgess (Artisan, 2011).

For spindle spinning we have been inspired by Bette Hochberg's booklets *Handspindles* (1977) and *Handspinners Handbook* (1980). They are available through the used book market. We also recommend *Respect the Spindle: Spin Infinite Yarns with One Amazing Tool* by Abby Franquemont (Krause Craft, 2009).

For researching and connecting to the Fibershed movement we recommend Rebecca Burgess' book *Fibershed: Growing a Movement of Farmers, Fashion Activists, and Makers for a New Textile Economy* (Chelsea Green Publishing, 2019), as well as visiting fibershed.org.

For publications on Rudolf Steiner's work and Waldorf education go to rsarchive.org, a free online library.

The texts from Louise van Blommestein's small book *Kuenstlerische Handarbeiten* (Artistic Handwork) (Philosophisch-Anthroposophischer Verlag Am Goetheanum 1934) can be found online in English translation as "Indications for Design in Handwork," parts 1 and 2, at waldorflibrary.org in the journal section. See *Child and Man* 31, no. 1 (January 1997) and 33, no. 2 (July 1999), https://www.waldorflibrary.org/journals/91-child-and-man/150-child-and-man.

References

On page 8, the poem "Song of the Sky Loom" is from Herbert Joseph Spinden's translation of *Songs of the Tewa* at sacred-texts.com/nam/sw/sot/sot33.htm.

On page 21, the epigraph to "Waldorf Education and the Handwork Curriculum" is from "Opening Address" in Rudolf Steiner's *Foundations of Human Experience* (Hudson, NY: Anthroposophic Press, 1996).

On pages 21 and 22, sketches are from Louise Van Blommestein's *Künstlerische Handarbeiten* (Artistic Handwork). See the link above, in "Recommended Resources."

For the quote from Hedwig Hauck on page 23, we used Hedwig Hauck's *Kunst und Handarbeit* (Handwork and Handicrafts), part 1, from indications by Rudolf Steiner, translated by Graham Rickett (London: Rudolf Steiner Press, 1968).

On page 24, the epigraph to "The Art of Clothing—Past, Present, and Future" is Rudolf Steiner's "Ecce Homo," the dedication to *Truth Wrought Words, Rightly-Spoken Words*, GA 40, December, 1923, Rudolf Steiner Archive, https://rsarchive.org/Articles/GA040/English/JR2023/index.html.

On page 24, the text cites *Elephants to Einstein*, a book based on Rudolf Steiner's discussions with workers at the Goetheanum in 1924 (London: Rudolf Steiner Press, 2009).

On page 28, the epigraph to "The Wonders of Knitting" is from "Lecture Seven, April 21, 1923," in Rudolf Steiner's *The Child's Changing Consciousness* (Hudson, NY: Anthroposophic Press, 1996).

On page 30, the quote from Dr. Hermann von Baravalle is from *Die Erscheinungen am Sternenhimmel* (Configurations in the Starry Heavens), translation by Renate Hiller.

On page 138, in "The Gestures and Tools of Hand Spinning," the quotes from Mahatma Ghandi are from "Ghandi Quotes on Khadi," accessed February 19, 2025, https://www.mkgandhi.org/swadeshi_khadi/khadiquotes.php.

On page 142, the epigraph to "The Magic of Color and the Process of Dyeing with Plants" is from *Colour, Healing, and the Human Soul: Understanding Colours and Using Them for Health and Therapy* by Gladys Mayer (Forest Row, UK: Rudolf Steiner Press, 2019).

www.ingramcontent.com/pod-product-compliance
Lightning Source LLC
Chambersburg PA
CBHW040929240426
43667CB00026B/2993